Sons of the American Revolution

The Lebanon War Office

Sons of the American Revolution

The Lebanon War Office

ISBN/EAN: 9783337125325

Printed in Europe, USA, Canada, Australia, Japan

Cover: Foto ©ninafisch / pixelio.de

More available books at **www.hansebooks.com**

THE LEBANON WAR OFFICE.

THE
HISTORY OF THE BUILDING,
AND
REPORT OF THE CELEBRATION
AT
LEBANON, CONN.,

FLAG DAY, JUNE 15, 1891.

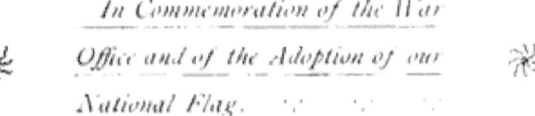

In Commemoration of the War Office and of the Adoption of our National Flag.

PUBLISHED BY THE
Connecticut Society of Sons of the American Revolution.
AND
SOLD FOR THE BENEFIT OF THE SOCIETY'S MEMORIAL FUND.

EDITED BY JONATHAN TRUMBULL.

HARTFORD, CONN.
PRESS OF THE CASE, LOCKWOOD & BRAINARD COMPANY.
1891.

Copyright, 1891,
By JONATHAN TRUMBULL.

CONTENTS.

Lebanon and the War Office
    Importance of Lebanon in Revolutionary times   5
    The early history of the War Office   6
    The Council of Safety, and its meetings at Lebanon   7
    The War Office after the Revolution   9
    Its conveyance to the Sons of the American Revolution   10
    Repairs and restorations   11
    Papers found in the building during repairs   12
    Ensign Moland's letter   14
    History of the writer's adventures   15
    Ralph Isaac's letter   16
    Gov. Franklin   16
    Treatment of Isaacs by the General Assembly and Council of Safety   17

The Celebration of the Restoration of the War Office
    Arrangements and general features of the celebration   20
    Address by Gen. Joseph R. Hawley   27

The Collation   30

Afternoon Exercises
    Prayer by Rev. William DeLoss Love   30
    Presentation of the War Office by Hon. Nathaniel B. Williams   31
    Acceptance by the President of the Connecticut Society Sons of the American Revolution   33
    Address by Mr. Erastus Geer   35
    Poem by Mr. Thomas S. Collier   38
    Oration by the Rev. Dr. Leonard W. Bacon   43
    Reading of Letters by the Hon. E. J. Hill   57
    Congratulatory Address by the Hon. Charles A. Russell   62
    Flag Day Address by Mr. Jonathan F. Morris   64
    Address by the Rev. Dr. Samuel G. Buckingham   74

Appendix
    Gov. Trumbull's Proclamation   83
    The Trumbull Papers   88
    Anecdote of a patriotic woman   89
    A Newspaper comment   90

Index   93

IN connection with this publication, it seems really necessary that a slight historical sketch of the War Office should be given, embodying such matters of interest as did not come within the scope of the various able and interesting addresses of the occasion. This report is, therefore, prefaced by the following sketch, which was read before the Connecticut Historical Society, Sept. 15, 1891. That society having joined in the celebration at Lebanon, it seemed appropriate that the historical portion of this work should be submitted to its criticism before publication, in order to avail of the authority which such criticism can give to any work of the kind. J. T.

LEBANON AND THE WAR OFFICE.

ALTHOUGH Lebanon appears to have been exceeded in population by thirteen of the seventy-six towns enumerated in the census of 1774, the excess was, in most cases, slight, and the population, 3,960, is, by no means, an adequate measure of the importance of the town in the days of the Revolution. In the grand list of 1775, but ten towns showed a higher valuation of taxable property. But most significant of all is the fact that, in the awards for services in the Lexington Alarm, but two towns in the State, Windham and Woodstock, were granted larger sums of money as their compensation.

The reasons for a service so largely in excess of any quota which Lebanon might have been called upon to furnish at this time seem evident. Here were the residence and home office of the only colonial governor who asserted the rights of his country as opposed to the oppressive measures of his king, which very fact must have given to that all-potent assemblage of the day, the town meeting, an inspiration and force which it might otherwise have lacked. Owing to the location of the town and the fact that the governor resided there, Lebanon must have been the place where the news from Boston was usually received in the exciting times which led up to the Revolution.

The limits of this publication prevent us from making extracts from the town records of these days, especially in the time of the non-importation agreements, the Port Bill, and the Boston massacre, records of proceedings and measures echoed and duplicated, no doubt, in many another Connecticut town, but peculiarly inspired in

Lebanon — seeming to-day almost ludicrously fervent in their expressions of "affectionate loyalty to his excellent Majesty," the acts of whose parliament they denounce in the most uncompromising terms. Such expressions of loyalty should not, however, be taken as a hypocritical cloak for the subsequent revolt, but rather as a *bona fide* endeavor to obtain rights which, had they been granted at the time, might have caused quite a difference in our present form of government.

In this atmosphere and on this soil of patriotism stood the humble little gambrel-roofed building which was the home office of the Governor; some rods from its present site, and facing the Colchester road near the northwest corner of its junction with Town street. It is impossible to determine the exact age of this building. It may have been, and probably was, the store of Governor Trumbull's father in 1732, the date which marks the beginning of the son's mercantile career; and it is more or less intimately connected with that career to the time of his failure in 1766 or thereabouts.

Owing to the public offices which Trumbull held during this period of thirty-four years, it is safe to assume that much business of a public as well as private character was transacted within this building during this time. Its importance in the history of our State and country begins more particularly with the year 1769, when, at the death of Governor Pitkin, Trumbull was elected as his successor, taking up, among other things, the important correspondence with William Samuel Johnson, who was then in England undertaking the settlement and management of the celebrated Mohegan case. The Mohegan case, however, sinks into insignificance during the time of Johnson's embassy; for while it was dragging its tedious course through the British tribunals from 1767 to June 11, 1771, the riots in Boston and the non-importation agreements of the colonies were leading to hot discussions and oppressive legislation in the British Parliament, which at last led to our independence in the war of the Revolution. Johnson faithfully attended these sessions of Parliament while patiently waiting the final issue of the Mohegan case. His letters to Governors Pitkin and Trumbull during this time show that he was then intelligently watching, and, so far as he could, influencing the action of Parliament in its all-important measures concerning the American Colonies. The letters of Trumbull to Johnson at this critical time are, with one exception, dated at Lebanon, and hardly could have been written elsewhere than in the private apartment of this little building where the writer had been accustomed to transact his business for some thirty years.

The interval from 1769 to 1775 is one in which much business of vital importance must have been transacted at the Governor's home office. The history of all that may have taken place there, beyond the correspondence just mentioned and the discussions to which this correspondence must have led, can only be supplied by conjecture. Lying, as Lebanon lay at the time, on the direct road to Boston, it is certain, as has been said, that, during this interval, many important despatches were received at this office, and that much serious and earnest counsel was held there regarding the alarming state of public affairs.

Soon after the Lexington Alarm, it became evident that the General Assembly must delegate its powers to provide for the sudden and imperative daily needs of the time. The following act was therefore passed at the May session of 1775:

"This Assembly do appoint the Honble Mathew Griswold Esqr, and the Honble Eliphalet Dyer, Jabez Huntington, and Samuel Huntington Esq^{rs}, William Williams, Nathaniel Wales jun^r, Jedidiah Elderkin, Joshua West, and Benjamin Huntington Esq^{rs}, a Committee to assist his Honor the Governor when the Assembly is not sitting, to order and direct the marches and stations of the inhabitants inlisted and assembled for the special defence of the Colony, or any part or parts of them, as they shall judge necessary, and to give order from time to time for furnishing and supplying said inhabitants with every matter and thing that may be needful to render the defence of the Colony effectual."

It will be seen at a glance that this act contemplated that the meetings of the committee should be held at Lebanon, three of its members besides the Governor being residents of that town, and the other members, with the exception of Deputy-Governor Griswold, being residents of the then adjoining towns of Norwich and Windham. This committee was kept in existence, by renewed acts of the General Assembly, during the entire war, with such extension of its powers and changes in its membership as appeared to be required. It soon became known as a council instead of a committee, being so named in the records of the General Assembly, as well as in the journal of its proceedings under its appointment by that body. This journal, with the exception of the record of a very few meetings, is complete to November, 1783, the original being in the custody of the State. The complete text of this journal is only printed to October, 1776, in the valuable Colonial Records, edited by Dr. Charles J. Hoadly.

A review of the number of meetings of the Council of Safety, of which abstracts were published by Hinman, has led the late Mr. Nathaniel H. Morgan to the estimate that, of the whole number of meetings during the war, some 1,200 in all, 1,145 were held in the War Office at Lebanon.

Of the proceedings at these meetings, it is, of course, impossible to give an adequate idea in this connection. The members of the Council of Safety may, perhaps, appropriately be called the minute-men of the General Assembly. Not only were they ready at all times for the arduous and important duties imposed upon them; but these duties made continual demands upon their time and energies. In the momentous month of July, 1776, eighteen meetings were held at Lebanon, and in the fol-

lowing month, sixteen, one of which was held on Sunday. The records of the Council tell, among other things, of the raising of troops, their apportionment to different fields of service, the fitting out of war vessels, the purchase and despatch of provisions and munitions of war, and the disposal of prisoners. Many of the distinguished officers of the time were present at these meetings or in private interviews with the Governor and members of his Council. The well-worn oaken floor of the War Office has doubtless been trodden by Washington, Sullivan, Knox, Parsons, Spencer, and by many of the officers among our French allies who were cantoned at Lebanon, or camped there on their marches during the years 1780 and 1781. Among these French officers may be mentioned Lafayette, Rochambeau, and the Duke de Lauzun. The many sudden and urgent calls of Washington for men, money, and materials in the dark days of the Revolution were met in the old War Office with that promptness and adequacy which have given to our commonwealth the historical title of the Provision State.

With the close of the Revolution in the victory of our arms came the close of the public career of Connecticut's war Governor and his War Office. The Governor saw the victory for which he had toiled and hoped and prayed, saw with it the completion of his life-work, and resigned his office to younger and less tired hands. After a time, the War Office passed into other ownerships. Removed a little from its original site, it filled, for a time, the modest function of a country store, and is still remembered as filling this function by some of the older inhabitants of Lebanon. Under another change of ownership, it was again removed to its present site, where, for a time, it was used as a dwelling-house; until at last it appeared to have outlived its usefulness. But during all this time its history was not forgotten. It was always known as the "War Office," and local tradition as well as written history told the story of the building. Whenever the occasional newspaper correspondent visited Lebanon, the building and its history were made the usually unfortunate victims of his pen. The varied and variously attired accounts of the building and its surroundings which have appeared in the metropolitan journals would form a little literature on the subject rather more amusing, and sometimes more provoking than accurate. Even romance has hovered about the old building in the story of Mistress Prudence Strong, printed some twenty years ago in the New York *Sun*, and largely copied by other papers of lesser note. The heroine appears to have been a mythical personage unknown to the town records or the families of Lebanon; while the hero, whose name may or may not be correctly given, was a French soldier, who, for some trifling lapse in duty, was sentenced by a court-martial to be shot as a deserter. The romance tells how Mistress Prudence Strong procured his pardon at the War Office from Rochambeau, how the pardon was entrusted to a sentry for delivery, and delivered too late. A French soldier of Lauzun's legion was certainly shot as a deserter at Lebanon; but beyond this fact, the romance of Mistress Prudence Strong appears to be romance, pure and simple.

During the ownership of Mrs. Bethiah H. Wattles, an attempt was made towards the repair, restoration, and custody of the War Office by the town, at the desire of its owner. The failure of this attempt reflects no discredit upon the people of Lebanon as a community, but goes to show, in a general way, that the town meeting of the present day is not the town meeting of the days of the Revolution, and usually yields surprises to the class of citizens composing the best and most broadly patriotic portion of the community who are absent from gatherings of the kind, or unprepared for the methods of opposition which they have to encounter. Probably for this reason, it is impossible, after considerable search, to find a case in which the preservation of a building of such historical interest, involving considerable expense and continual care, has ever been undertaken by a town or a

small local organization. The proper custodian, unless it be the State itself, is an organization of the State at large, whose scope and purposes contemplate work of this kind. Such an organization, the Connecticut Society of Sons of the American Revolution had grown to be in the winter of 1890-91, at which time Mr. Frank Farnsworth Starr was appointed by the society's board of managers to visit Lebanon, and make such arrangements as could be made for the preservation of the War Office. His explanation of the nature of the organization he represented and of the object of his visit resulted in the prompt execution of a deed of gift of the building, and a suitable portion of the land upon which it is located, to the society by Mrs. Wattles, the owner, a lady ninety-one years of age, who, with the relatives composing her household, had long cherished the design of placing the building beyond the danger of destruction. The sole condition of the deed was that the building should be properly repaired, and kept in repair in the future. This condition the society gladly and gratefully accepted, and appointed its president to investigate the condition of the building, and, subsequently, to arrange for and superintend the necessary repairs and restorations. The oak framework, with the exception of the sills, was found to be in a good state of preservation. Traces of the original partitions, windows, and doors were also found to be so plainly marked that the restoration could really be made complete. The work was commenced early in May, by Mr. Charles Morgan Williams of Norwich, who planned and carried out the entire undertaking.

A completely new stone foundation was laid under the building, the decayed sills were replaced by new timber, the sides and roof were newly shingled, the original partitions, doors, and windows were restored, and an entirely new chimney of the colonial type was substituted for the very small one which had evidently been placed in the building as a substitute for the original chimney. Old-fashioned stone fire-places form a marked feature of the restored chimney. These fire-places were procured by Mr. Williams, with some difficulty, from buildings in Lebanon which had either fallen down from their age, or had outlived their usefulness. Andirons made by a Lebanon blacksmith in the days of the Revolution were presented by Miss Dutton, forming, with the old iron cranes, a complete outfit for these important features of the interior.

In the romance to which reference has been made, it is intimated that certain documents of importance were concealed by Mistress Prudence Strong within the walls of the building. While the story was known to be a romance, this intimation served, at least, as a reminder that it would be well to make a careful search for relics wherever opportunity offered. This search was, at first, rewarded only by the finding of fragments of papers among the solid mass of oat-husks, nutshells, rags, and other materials which, at unknown times during the past century, had formed the nests of rats and squirrels under the upper flooring. These fragments were as interesting in their indications as they were provoking in their incompleteness. They appeared to be scraps of old muster-rolls, with here and there a complete name, fragments of old newspapers, and bits of correspondence, one of which, in the Governor's handwriting, reads thus:

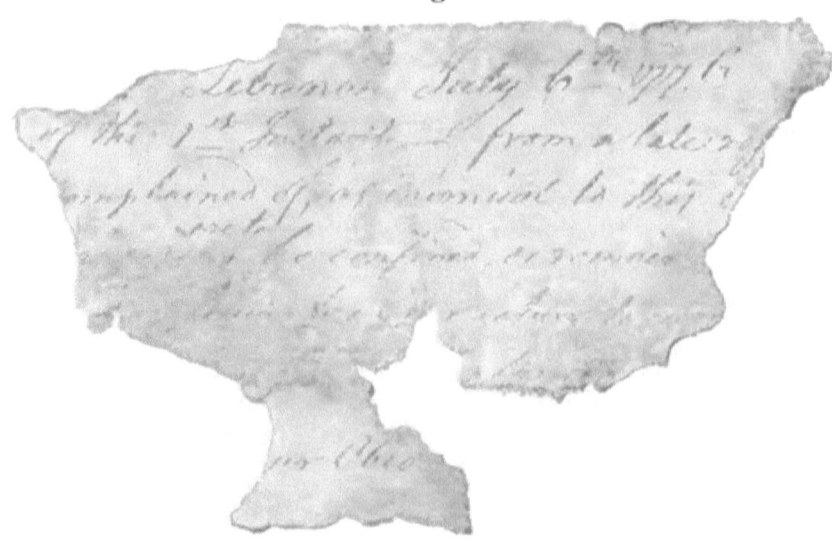

Two days before the date of this fragment, Governor William Franklin of New Jersey had been sent to the care of Governor Trumbull, as a prisoner, and had asked to be paroled in New Jersey. Possibly this fragment was a part of the correspondence regarding Franklin's parole.

About a week after the discovery of these fragments, some papers were found in a wonderfully good state of preservation, considering the fact that the rats and squirrels had been their custodians for, perhaps, a century. The following is a list of the most important of these papers:

Bond of Noah Dewey, Jan. 8, 1740, to "the Governor and Company of the English Colony of Connecticutt" for the sum of eighteen shillings.

Letter of John Ledyard, Hartford, "to Col^r. Jona Trumble, merchant, at Lebanon," Nov. 20, 1762.

Official census-return of the "Town of Glassenbury on the first of January, 1774."

Letter of R. Isaacs, New Haven, "to his Excellency Govr. Franklin at Middletown," Aug. 7, 1776.

Petition of Ens. Joseph Moland, Nov. 25, 1776, asking the Governor for release from imprisonment.

Attested copy of vote of a town meeting at New Haven, December 9, 1776, asking for small arms, field-pieces, etc., for the defense of the town.

Full copy of "*Freeman's Journal*" Numb. 1, April 25, 1781.

The interest in these papers is, of course, heightened by the singular circumstances under which they were discovered. They were, perhaps, mislaid, some of them being regarded as unimportant at the time; yet it is difficult to conceive how certain papers covering a range of forty-one years, received at this office at various times during that period, should have been stowed away in one place in the building. Perhaps when the Governor was selecting matter among his papers, as he did at one time, for the use of future historians, these documents were discarded by him as unnecessary in the valuable collection which his son David presented, in 1795, to the Massachusetts Historical Society.* Being so discarded, the rats probably took possession of them, and laid them by for future use as building material of their own. But had the rats been infected with the same regard for the chronicler of the future which actuated the Governor at the time, they hardly could have made a more appropriate selection for the purpose of confirming the outline already given of the history of the building during the most important period of its existence.

The bond of Noah Dewey carries us back to the year 1740, when Trumbull, then a man of thirty, occupied the position of "Assistant" in the General Assembly, and was at the same time engaged in mercantile pursuits. This bond pertained to the business of the State, and was witnessed and perhaps procured by Trumbull, who, it should be remembered, spelled his name Trumble up to the year 1766, when his son's researches in the Herald's office caused him to adopt the present spelling. The letter of John Ledyard relates entirely to matters of personal business at a time when Ledyard was a partner in the business then carried on.

A fragment of a newspaper, not mentioned in the above list, is probably of the date of 1763, and shows that the news of that important time was read and discussed in the War Office.

The three papers bearing the date 1776 relate, evidently, to business of the Council of Safety; and, as they refer to a time every moment and circumstance of which is interesting to the historian and to the patriot, we reproduce, first for its quaintness, and for the reason that its story has been already told in the publications of the Connecticut Historical Society, the petition of Ensign Joseph Moland.

* See Appendix p. 88.

To
His Honor Jon.ᵗʰ Trumbull Esq.ʳ
Governor of Connecticut

Eng Lane & Morton
Nov. 25, 1774
Wilton

Sir

The Slavery you have now heard the Cause of my Confinement establishes the likely to lay it before you and am convinced that after perusing it you will think that my being confined August 29th is more than I ought to have suffered had I been guilty in the fullest sence of what is laid to my Charge — — On the Evening of the 19th Augt as I was walking through the Kitchen at M.r Kraus's Inn Stoken Tom Sleight, I think, my him against a Chair upon which I demanded I vow and Softly replied through to the Garden, on my return M.r Kraus called out & Told him to which I answered, whether he then deserved more for a Rascal Naskid it that was a way to answer — I then went into the Room where he was sitting and asked him what he wanted — he then answered me a second time for a Rascal bird and it was not the feature moved him I had not him Ill upon which I struck & Clubbed him & was going to make a second Stroke at him when his Wife came between us and received it in her Face which was intirely by accident & indeed the only thing I am sorry for —

To
The Honorable Ja.s Grimball Esq.r
Governor of Connecticut

Nov. 28
Geo Allen
1795

of no moment. I was next day sent for by no less
... Mess.rs Payne & Wadsworth, who after hearing
with Patie[n]ce was committed to them. I knew where it seemes
they intend keeping me until Exchanged — At Face &
a Vole force. Mr Body informing me I could not
expect to be enlarged unless I made an Apology to
Mr J. Mr Rice and the Committee with the fullest
assurances that any Confinement had worked a reform
whereon me & that I would not do so any more —
This Sir is the state of my Case — as to making an
Apology to a Man who was the agresor I cannot think
of doing it. — I am very willing to give my
Parole with Assurances to the Committee of not breaking
the Public Peace & shall expect at the same time
I am not to be insulted by People of the Town &
no notice taken of it — which I have hitherto experienced
I have the honor to be Sir
Your Most Ob.t Hum Serv.t
Jos. Moland

From researches made by Mr. Jonathan F. Morris of Hartford, it appears that this Ensign Moland was one of the officers of the Seventy-sixth regiment, captured at Ticonderoga May 10, 1775, and brought to Hartford, where he was paroled in company with his fellow officers, Major Skene, Captain Delaplace, and Ensign Rotton.

From the diary of Major French, who was also among the numerous prisoners under parole at Hartford at the time this letter was written, it appears that there were continual demonstrations of enmity on the part of the people of Hartford against these prisoners, which demonstrations may have had something to do with Moland's attitude towards his landlord. The diary of Major French from January 1 to September 13, 1776, is printed in full in Vol. I of the Collections of the Connecticut Historical Society. The story of Moland's unfortunate collision with the chair, and subsequently with his landlord and landlady, is quite feelingly told in this diary, under date of August 19, 1776, with comments by the writer regarding the summary proceedings by which Moland was consigned to "durance vile."

In company with Major French and three others, Moland made his escape from "goal" on the 15th of November, 1776, but was captured with his comrades at Branford and again imprisoned. French, Moland, and one other made their final escape December 27, 1776, after which time, so far as can be ascertained, the name of Ensign Joseph Moland is unknown to history. The journal of the Council of Safety makes no mention of his petition for release. The date of this petition is removed from the original, but the paper is docketed November 25, 1776, which, as it seems, was ten days after his first escape, which was probably known to the Council of Safety at the time. The name of Moland appears, however, in the journal of this body at an earlier date, at which time, upon his arrival at Hartford, his petition to be paroled in company with his fellow prisoners was granted.

Another of these letters which requires more than a passing glance, and is interesting on account of the history of the person to whom it is addressed, and of the person by whom it was written, is the letter directed
" To
            " His Excelency Govr Franklin
                              att
" Per   Middletown.
    " Mr. J. Perit."

Governor Franklin of New Jersey, to whom this letter is addressed, is so well known to history that it is hardly necessary to give more than a reminding sketch of his career at the time this letter was written. Unlike his patriotic sire, the illustrious Benjamin Franklin, he is described in the journal of the Council of Safety as " a virulent enemy to this country." He arrived at Lebanon on the 4th of July, 1776, under guard, having been consigned by the authorities of New Jersey to the care of Governor Trumbull, with the request that he be paroled as a prisoner. After a discussion in which it is said Franklin's language and demeanor were by no means suited to the temper of the Governor and his Council, he was paroled at Wallingford, and about two weeks later at Middletown, where, no doubt, he received the letter from Mr. Isaacs. On the 30th of April, 1777, orders were received from Congress to place Franklin in close confinement without access to writing materials. He was, accordingly, sent to Litchfield jail. It is, of course, impossible to say when and how this letter of Isaacs came into possession of the Council of Safety. Although it is most natural to infer that it was found among Franklin's effects at the time of his imprisonment, still, from what happened to the writer soon after the letter reached its destination, it may have been intercepted and seized at about that time.

New Haven Augst: 76 —

Your Excellency
Govr Trumbull

R. Nickes

By Cap.t Jn.o Starr I had the Pleasure to forward you a Case of Oyl and a &c. from Turn. I wish I could have Serv.d you better, those are not in my L.r wed. I had it from M.r Smith Son indeed to M.rs Sears and gave him 18/— M.rs D. Lyman has half doz.n of Stockings which are coarse if they will do be so kind as to let me hear by the Bearer who is Brother to M.rs Jn.o Breed and will return here in a few days.

We have Certain News arrived from N. York that 100 Sail of Ships Arrived at the Island which General Howe has taken possession of, and that yesterday a Fleet was seen off the South side of Long Island Standing towards the Hook — I beg you will be so kind as to Let me know if Lady Franklin is coming this way, I shall esteem it a particular Honour to wait on Her — My sincerest wishes attend you and believe me to be with Great Truth & Regard

Your Excellencys
Most H.ble Son.t
R. Silves

It appears that the writer, Ralph Isaacs, was by no means exempt from the inevitable lot of tories, or suspected tories, in our State at this time. September 27, 1776, upon a memorial of some citizens of New Haven, the Council of Safety directed that this Isaacs and some other suspected persons be cited to appear before the General Assembly at its coming session in October, to make answer to the charges against them. At the hearing, it appeared that "Mr. Isaacs had been frequently at Gov. Brown's* quarters, and seemed to be pleased in the company of Tories," that he had made derogatory remarks regarding the conduct of the Continental troops at the battle of Long Island, and that he had sent some fine blackfish to Governor Brown at Middletown.

Isaacs and Capt. Abiather Camp were found guilty of the charges laid against them, and were removed to the Society of Eastbury in Glastenbury, there to remain under careful surveillance and restrictions. Dec. 11, 1776, the Council of Safety allowed Isaacs, upon his petition, to be removed to more commodious quarters in Durham, owing to his ill health. During the following January, a complaint was sent to the Council of Safety by the committee of inspection for the town of Durham, stating that Isaacs was a dangerous person to be at large and to retail rum, whereupon further restrictions were laid upon him by the Council, which body ordered that his rum be seized and sold for the benefit of the State. At various other times the name of Isaacs appears as a petitioner to the General Assembly. At the October session of 1777, he was allowed to appear in courts where he had action depending for trial, upon condition of taking the oath of fidelity. At last, his checkered career as a tory prisoner in various towns of the State ended in his release by the General Assembly at its special session in January, 1778, on which occasion

---

*Governor Montford Brown of New Providence, Bahama Islands, captured at the taking of the island and sent to Connecticut as a prisoner of war.

he showed that he had taken the oath of fidelity, and that he had done and should continue to do much to aid the cause of the United States.

Although the journal of the Council of Safety makes no mention of the letter which Isaacs wrote Gov. Franklin in August, 1776, and although this letter was so neglected that it reposed peacefully in the old War Office for nearly one hundred and fifteen years, there can be no doubt that it was quite keenly perused by the Council of Safety at the time of its receipt, and that it may have had more to do with the trials and tribulations of Ralph Isaacs than we are now able to prove. What may have been the effect of reading the title "His Excelency," even though it was spelled with one l, as applied to a tory governor, it is difficult to say. When we imagine the punctilious Huntingtons and others of the council discussing this point at a time when *His Honor* was a sufficient title for their own patriot governor, we must imagine that their righteous indignation found vent in a way by no means agreeable to Mr. Isaacs.*

Of the other papers discovered in the War Office, it is only necessary to mention the petition of the town meeting of New Haven, Dec. 9, 1776, asking for arms and for the adoption of measures for the defense of the town. Although this petition is not specifically mentioned in the journal of the Council of Safety, that body appears to have had it under consideration at its meeting four days after the date of the petition, at which meeting it was voted that six field pieces captured from the *Minerva* be fitted with carriages for the use of New Haven, and that the militia under Col. Thompson be thoroughly organized for the defense of that town.

The process of reading between the lines in a statement of plain facts and tedious routine like the journal of the Council of Safety is a dangerous and often misleading process; yet, if the patient and scientific his-

---

* The title *His Excellency* was adopted in the following year, 1777, as the title of the Governor of Connecticut, by act of the General Assembly.

torian of to-day should apply it to this journal, he would, no doubt, be able to make a volume or two which, while it would form a lasting and fitting tribute to the old War Office, would also throw much new light upon the history of our State in the days of the Revolution. It is to be hoped that the valuable Colonial Records already printed will be followed by the publication of the entire journal of the General Assembly and Council of Safety, as a continuation of this work.

A new era in the history of the Lebanon War Office has now commenced, and has been celebrated by the Sons of the American Revolution and by the Connecticut Historical Society in a way that appears to make it worthy of a carefully printed report, to which the remainder of this publication is devoted.

THE CELEBRATION

OF THE

RESTORATION OF THE WAR OFFICE.

AT its annual meeting, May 11, 1891, the Connecticut Society of Sons of the American Revolution voted that a celebration should be held at Lebanon, to commemorate the completion of the repairs and restoration of the War Office, and to re-dedicate the building to public uses. The anniversary of the adoption of our National Flag was selected for this purpose, with a view to establishing an observance of the day, for which the society has adopted the title of *Flag Day*. As the anniversary fell on Sunday of this year, it was found necessary to hold the celebration on the following Monday, June 15th. The Connecticut Historical Society was invited to join in this celebration ; and accordingly selected the day as its annual "field day," for that purpose.

On the part of the Society of Sons of the Revolution, the following committees of Norwich members were appointed by the president to complete the arrangements for the celebration :

General Committee.— Mr. Adams P. Carroll, Chairman ; Mr. Burrell W. Hyde, Secretary ; Dr. Leonard B. Almy, Major B. P. Learned, Messrs. Charles R. Butts, George C. Raymond, and J. L. W. Huntington.

On Programme.— Hon. Jeremiah Halsey, Chairman ; Dr. Robert P. Keep and Mr. Frank J. Leavens.

The general committee at once sent two of its members with the president of the society to arrange with the residents of Lebanon the details of the celebration. They were most cordially met by a number of Lebanon's leading citizens, in consultation with whom plans were arranged for the leading features of the occasion. They insisted upon offering to the two societies and their guests an ample collation, and made many valuable suggestions regarding the general arrangements. The spirit of the people of Lebanon regarding the proposed celebration is, perhaps, best illustrated by a remark made by one of their number. It was suggested that some of the residents who might be called upon to assist in the arrangements might not be able to give up the time which it would be necessary to devote to the work on the day; to which the reply came in no uncertain tones: "If any man in Lebanon cannot give up the day to this celebration, the town has no use for him." The residents at once took up the work which devolved upon them, placing it in charge of the following committees, appointed at a meeting of the citizens of Lebanon, held in the Town Hall, May 30, 1891.

CHAIRMAN, Hon. J. C. Crandall.
SECRETARY AND TREASURER, N. C. Barker.

COMMITTEES.

To deliver Keys of the War Office to the Society of Sons of the American Revolution — Hon. N. B. Williams.

On Transportation from Chestnut Hill Station — John H. Avery, John S. King, W. B. Loomis.

On Transportation from North Franklin Station — Frank K. Noyes, Edgar J. Tucker, Charles J. Abell.

On Transportation from Willimantic — W. F. Gates.

On Care of Teams — A. R. Post, Clark Standish, L. P. Smith, Charles Sweet, Jr.

Building Platform and Tables — A. R. Post, W. A. Wetmore, C. L. Pitcher, C. Sweet, Jr., E. W. Hewitt, Sands Throop.

Dishes — Frank P. Fowler.

To Solicit Funds — Frank P. Fowler, South Society;

Erastus Geer, Goshen Society; George A. Mills, Exeter Society; W. F. Gates, North Society.

To Solicit Refreshments:

District No. 1,	{	Mrs. W. F. Gates.
	{	Mrs. Edward Moffitt.
" No. 2,	{	Mrs. Charles Robinson.
	{	Mrs. R. P. Burgess.
" No. 3,	{	Miss Annie E. Briggs.
	{	Miss Cecil Browning.
" No. 4,	{	Mrs. John Clark.
	{	Mrs. Henry Clark.
" No. 5,	{	Miss Hattie J. Manley.
	{	Mrs. John H. Avery.
" No. 6,	{	Miss Helen O. Prindle.
	{	Miss Hattie E. Hewitt.
" No. 7,	{	Mrs. F. K. Noyes.
	{	Mrs. G. W. Lyman.
" No. 8,	{	Mrs. Phebe C. Irish.
	{	Miss Minnie Hoxie.
" No. 9,		Mrs. Andrew Waterman.
" No. 10,	{	Mrs. Charles Winchester.
	{	Mrs. William W. Gillett.
" No. 11,	{	Mrs. Erastus Geer.
	{	Mrs. Charles Taylor.
" No. 12,	{	Miss Masey E. Stark.
	{	Mrs. James Y. Thomas.
" No. 13,	{	Mrs. A. G. Kneeland.
	{	Mrs. L. A. Spaulding.
" No. 14,	{	Mrs. George A. Mills.
	{	Mrs. Myron Abell.
" No. 15,	{	Mrs. George A. Nye.
	{	Mrs. Frederick J. Brown.
" No. 16,	{	Mrs. Edward A. Stiles.
	{	Miss Walden.

Coffee — L. P. Smith.

To Prepare Tables — Miss Maria F. Barker, Miss Ellen C. Williams.

To Set Food on Tables, Town Hall — Mrs. H. D. Stebbins, Mrs. E. A. Stiles, Mrs. G. A. Mills, Mrs. G. A. Nye, Mrs. C. S. Briggs, Mrs. L. H. Randall, Mrs. Edward Gibbs, Mrs. James Y. Thomas, Mrs. Wm. Robinson, Mrs. Hobart McCall, Mrs. William Taylor, Mrs. Nelson Taylor, Miss Louise Robinson.

At Brick Church — Mrs. L. P. Loomis, Mrs. R. P. Burgess, Mrs. W. B. Avery, Mrs. J. H. Avery, Mrs. C. H. Peckham, Mrs. Nancy E. Pettis, Mrs. L. L. Lyman, Miss S. M. Dolbeare.

To Hang Flags — Joe Stedman.

The society's committee on programme decided upon the following order of exercises:

Lebanon War Office Celebration.

FLAG DAY, 1891.

PROGRAM.

11:30 A. M. to 1 P. M.

Flag-raising at the War Office and at the residence of Mrs. Wattles, its donor, which was the Governor's residence during the Revolution.

Music.

Address by Gen. Joseph R. Hawley.

Reception and Loan Exhibition at the War Office.

1 P. M.

Dinner-call by Drum Corps, followed by Collation, by invitation, to the Connecticut Society of Sons of the American Revolution; the Connecticut Historical Society, and their guests.

2 P. M.

Assembly-call by the Drum Corps, and procession to the War Office and Speakers' stand.

2:30 P. M.

Prayer by the Rev. William DeLoss Love.

Presentation of the War Office by Mr. Nathaniel B. Williams.

Response by the President of the Society.

Music.

Poem by Mr. Thomas S. Collier.

Address by the Rev. Dr. Leonard W. Bacon.

Music, "America," sung by all.

Addresses by invited guests.

Benediction.

Tubbs' Military Band of Norwich, twenty-five pieces, and the Nathan Hale Drum Corps of South Coventry, fourteen pieces, were engaged to furnish the instrumental music of the programme.

The 15th of June was a cloudless and intensely hot day. The early trains brought to Lebanon a throng of members of the Society of Sons of the Revolution and others, who were readily provided with transportation to the center of attraction, the War Office, some three miles from the nearest railway station. On the road the old cemetery was passed, containing the tomb where Governor Trumbull and other members of his family, including his son-in-law, William Williams, a signer of the Declaration of Independence, are buried. The tomb had been recently repaired by descendants of these ancestors, and was decorated with flags by the Lebanon committee. Arriving at the Green, a large concourse of people were found assembled at an early hour. The town was in holiday attire, and the houses gaily decorated with bunting and devices. Near the town-house on the Green a large flag extended across the street bore, in conspicuous letters, the words,

"WELCOME, SONS OF THE REVOLUTION."

A mound on the Green shows all that is left of a large brick oven in which the cooking was done for the huzzars of Lauzun's legion when they were quartered at Lebanon in the winter of 1781. At this mound, and at the "barracks lot" near by, the French and American flags were displayed. The grave of the deserter who was shot under sentence of a French court martial was marked by a French flag.

By ten o'clock the throng had increased to such an extent that it was decided to vary the programme by admitting visitors at once to the War Office for registration and for examination of the loan exhibition. The register was placed upon the broad arm of a chair which once belonged to Governor Trumbull. Quill pens made by Mr. Nathaniel B. Williams from Lebanon geese were used by those who registered their names. The inkstand was one which had been made of a piece of soapstone by Dr. Nott. The first name upon the register was that of the donor of the building, Mrs. Bethiah H. Wattles, aged ninety-one. The band discoursed its music while the visitors examined the exhibition of relics and curiosities which had been carefully collected and arranged under the supervision of Miss Mary H. Dutton. This exhibit consisted of specimens of old-time needle-work, products of the spinning-wheel, old firearms, sabres and rapiers, pictures, china, old volumes, documents, and utensils, forming a most interesting and valuable collection, of which it is impossible to furnish a catalogue in this connection.

The speakers' stand had been erected under the shade of the maple trees in the ample space in front of the residence of Mrs. Wattles, which, from its history, formed an attraction equal to the War Office itself. This house was hospitably thrown open to the numerous visitors who wished to cross the threshold of the mansion where Governor Trumbull resided in the days of the Revolution, and its dooryard was thronged with those who availed themselves of the numerous seats provided under the welcome shade.

Owing to a delay of nearly an hour in the arrival of the train from Hartford, it was impossible to commence the exercises until about twelve o'clock. Up to this time the attendance had been steadily increasing by the arrival of the train from New Haven with a delegation of over one hundred, and by the continual influx of visitors in carriages from Norwich, Willimantic, Windham, and other towns. The train from Hartford brought the members of the Connecticut Historical Society, many of whom were also members of the Sons of the American Revolution, which society also furnished a large delegation from Hartford.

Lineal descendants of Jonathan Trumbull and General Jabez Huntington stood ready to hoist the flag at the given signal, to signify that Trumbulls and Huntingtons could still pull together at the War Office as in the days of '76. At the roll of the drums the flag, with its thirteen stars, floated over the building. A few minutes later another flag bearing, in large letters, the words,

"BROTHER JONATHAN,"

was displayed from the residence of Mrs. Wattles. "The Star Spangled Banner" was admirably rendered as a solo by Mrs. Favor of Lebanon, to the accompaniment of the band, the audience joining heartily in the chorus under the leadership of Prof. Favor.

General Hawley, having been conducted to the platform by President Trumbull, was introduced by him in the following words:

Ladies and Gentlemen: We are honored to-day by the presence of one whose career as hero and statesman connects him so intimately with our country's flag that we might search in vain for one who could more fittingly utter the sentiments which the sight of our national ensign inspires. I have the honor and pleasure to announce an address by General Joseph R. Hawley.

General Hawley's appearance was greeted with loud and prolonged applause.

He spoke as follows:

GENERAL HAWLEY'S ADDRESS.

[From the Hartford *Courant* of June 16, 1891.]

Mr. Chairman, Ladies and Gentlemen:

This is an occasion unique in the history of a nation which is, in itself, remarkable. I am told that this is the first time a flag was ever raised over this War Office. In the stirring times of the Revolution they were too busy to attend to it. We look on our country as comparatively new, but that flag is one of the oldest of flags. The

British flag in its present form is of later birth. Our flag is a flag of exceeding beauty. Perhaps a stranger would not think so, but to us at least it is beautiful with its dear associations. It is now the flag of a nation of sixty-two millions of people, next to China and Russia, the largest nation of the world, and a nation which is making rapid progress.

It has been said that we boast too much, but now men are beginning to look back and to depreciate us. Nevertheless there is nowhere in the world a wiser creation of man than the revised statutes of the United States of America. Our creed is as near perfect as human thought can make it. I will be glad to have any man compare the list of presidents of this country with the kings and queens of any other nation. For wisdom and fidelity to duty our presidents have far eclipsed the royalty of other nations.

There is no government that has lived these two hundred and fifty years with so excellent a body of laws and so few changes. By the wisdom of Winthrop we obtained from Charles I. a charter which allowed us virtually a republican form of government. No government in Europe or elsewhere has continued with so little change since. To what do we owe all this? The discussion of that history would take too long. But I will say that one thing to which we owe it in large part is the organization of the township, a complete little republic in itself, and this township was formed around a church. The minister was a leader of the flock not only in religion but in politics and various matters of everyday life. Four men were indispensable in the formation of the Yankee township. They were the minister, the schoolmaster, the first selectman, and the captain of the militia company.

In the French war there were 32,000 separate enlistments from Connecticut. These men did not fight at the command of a king; they went at the request of the governor. Among all those who had a share in the building up of this commonwealth no one had a greater part than Jonathan Trumbull. He was an excellent governor. He was a born diplomatist. In private life he was a fine old gentleman with a bearing and courtesy that brought to him the love of all. He was a man of activity during that French war. There he stands as the only governor who marched his people into the war and kept them there till the war was over. It was wonderful what qualities of statesmanship were bred in these hills. He was practically the secretary of the navy and the War of the Revolution was won in a large measure by the navy.

The whole State owes you thanks, Sons of the Revolution, for what you are doing here. Some of us have been getting hungry for some real American doctrine. We welcome the emigrants, all who are willing to become American citizens, to bear arms for the country and to obey our laws. But many come only to better their own material condition, not recognizing that liberty is not license. There is plenty for this society to do. There are many old relics to be preserved. How strange that the State has not before this taken steps to have this old office preserved. Here was where Trumbull had his headquarters to watch over the interests of the nation. What a noble history! I believe it is given to departed saints to know what is done on earth. Then the old governor must be here on this occasion. He will be pleased, but he will wonder why this was not done long before. The future looks bright, and greater glories than any of those gone by are yet to come to this greatest country of the world.

This address was received with close attention by an audience of about two thousand people, who frequently interrupted it with applause.

A meeting of the board of managers had, meanwhile, been held, at which meeting thirty-three members were added to the Society of Sons of the American Revolution, upon applications previously approved by the

Registrar. At this meeting, a flag was presented to the board by Mr. Jonathan F. Morris, and was adopted by a vote of the board as the flag of the Society. This flag is a white field with a blue carton or union in the upper staff corner. These colors, blue and white, were the colors of Washington's Life Guard, whose uniform was a blue coat, trimmed with white, white waistcoat and knee-breeches.

The hour of one o'clock having arrived, the drum-corps sounded its call, and headed a long and informal procession for its short march to the town hall and the church near by, at both of which places an ample collation had been provided by the people of Lebanon; so ample that it sufficed not only for the members of the two societies and their guests, to the number of more than four hundred, but also for visitors who were not so fortunate as to wear the badge of either society, to whom also, to the number of three hundred or more, a cordial invitation was extended and accepted, to partake of the good things which Lebanon hospitality had provided. The dining-rooms were tastefully decorated, and the wants of guests were promptly supplied by a number of the ladies and gentlemen of Lebanon, many of whom deprived themselves of the pleasure of attending the exercises, in order to dispense the hospitalities of the occasion.

At two o'clock, the drums and fifes sounded the signal for assembling at the speakers' stand; and at half-past two, the exercises of the afternoon were opened with the following prayer by the Rev. William DeLoss Love, Chaplain of the Connecticut Society of Sons of the American Revolution:

Almighty God, Thou Father of all mankind, made manifest in Jesus Christ Thy Son, we adore and worship Thee. Thou didst make a covenant of freedom with our fathers when Thou broughtest them over the seas to these blessed shores. Here they raised their holy altars and taught their children to love liberty and revere the truth. And in the days of their conflict, Thou didst take command of their armies and gavest them the victory. We bless thee for their memories. Especially do we acknowledge Thy guidance in the life of him to whom it was given here in this historic spot to spend and be spent for his country. Thou didst raise him up, and in Thy time, when he had seen the reward of his labors, Thou didst gather him to his fathers in peace. We remember also with gratitude to Thee those patriotic men and women who upheld his hands in the day of conflict until the going down of the sun. O Almighty God, we their sons and daughters, having received at Thy hand a goodly heritage, humbly beseech Thee to instruct us in our duty as citizens that we may maintain the freedom established through their hardships endured and their blood shed. May we love righteousness and hate iniquity, and recognize Thee as our lawgiver and Thy blessed Son as our Redeemer.

Grant Thy providential guidance in all public affairs. Bless Thy servant the chief magistrate of these United States, our judges, Congress, and the governments of the several commonwealths. Unite us as one people, knowing no other land to call our own than this, and preserve our nation until kings and empires have an end, and Thy kingdom alone endureth, eternal in the heavens.

This we humbly ask through Jesus Christ Thy Son. Amen.

At the conclusion of this prayer, Mr. Nathaniel B. Williams of Lebanon arose and presented the War Office to the Society in the following address:

FORMAL PRESENTATION OF THE WAR OFFICE BY THE HON. N. B. WILLIAMS.

As we look at yonder flag with its thirteen stars floating in the breeze, it carries our minds back to the early history of this country, especially that period covered by the American Revolution.

Our relations to our mother country are more or less familiar to us all. When our ancestors first landed on

Plymouth Rock, and for a long time thereafter, they had no idea of separating their relation from Great Britain. But, as time wore on, her measures grew more and more oppressive; unjust requirements were constantly increasing, privileges to which they had a just right were constantly diminishing until at last the yoke became too galling for our fathers to submit to and still maintain their honor and self-respect as men.

After making appeal after appeal for redress — but all in vain then followed the Declaration of Independence, July 4, 1776. It was easy to make the declaration, but it was a mighty undertaking to maintain it, and this they fully understood when they pledged their lives, fortune, and sacred honor to the cause.

The foe was strong, our numbers comparatively few, resources limited, traitors numerous. Under such circumstances to succeed needed sound judgment, wise counsel, iron will, and an unbounded determination, all of which " Brother Jonathan " possessed during the trying years of the Revolution, and his ability to impart the same to others made him a power in maintaining our independence and in laying the foundation for the best government that the sun ever shone upon!

Another point necessary in maintaining our independence was concert of action, and the War Office was the great center of attraction from which such an influence arose, and its associations in this respect are calculated to touch the heart of every patriot. It was in that building that George Washington often met his bosom friend, our first war governor, and the only one in thirteen colonies in whom he could place implicit confidence. In that office they matured plans for future action. It was there that important war measures originated, dispatches were sent to the army, reports returned, and the war council held over one thousand sessions.

During some of the dark days of the Revolution, so dark as to be depressing to ordinary minds, it was the inspiring words that went forth from this council —

who believed their cause was the cause of God — that gave hope and cheer to the army and renewed courage to trust in Him who overrules all events, to keep their "powder dry" and "fight on, to victory or to death."

It was military headquarters for this part of the country, and its floors have been trodden by Washington, Trumbull, Adams — Samuel and John — Jefferson, Putnam, Franklin, Knox, and many others of note, both of this country and France.

The War Office was the center of influence to keep the fires of the Revolution burning, and this vast assembly shows that it will take more than another century to kill out the fire that burned in the bosoms of the patriots of '76.

I rejoice that there is a society called the "Sons of the American Revolution," formed for the purpose of perpetuating the memory of their fathers and preserving as memorials those relics that are connecting links with the revolution, and it affords me great pleasure, in behalf of Mrs. Wattles, the donor of the War Office, to present to the Society, through their president, Mr. Trumbull, the key of said office. I do not ask you to keep it in a state of preservation, for what you have already done and the fact that the blood of the Revolutionary fathers flows in your veins is sufficient guarantee for the future.

This Office withstood the storm of the Revolution; it saw the birth of this nation; it has defied the storms and tempests of more than one hundred and sixty years, and there let it stand as a memorial of the past, and an educator for the present and future generations, teaching them that the wise and good may die, but they are not forgotten!

The president of the society, Mr. Jonathan Trumbull, responded in the following words:

The Connecticut Society of Sons of the American Revolution gratefully accepts the trust which is implied in your conveyance of the time-honored War Office, in profound consciousness of all that this trust signifies.

It is not in words that we can convey to you a sense of this consciousness. To thank the donor for the spirit which has prompted the gift; to thank the people of this historic town for their generous and hearty coöperation in our attempts to honor the gift as it deserves, would be a mockery. Patriotism is not a thing for which one American may thank another; not a valuable commodity which can be passed over from an individual or a community to an organization like ours as a matter of compliment. It is patriotism alone which has manifested itself in the gift, and in all that the people of Lebanon have done in connection with it. We honor that sentiment too deeply to think of requiting it by empty words. We honor it in the venerable lady who has intrusted to us the completion of a design she has so long cherished; we honor it in the members of her family who have so effectively promoted and contributed to this purpose; and we honor it in the people of this town of Lebanon where patriotism always has shown itself, and always will show itself to be native to the soil.

As the result of a prompt and generous recognition of the character and spirit of our organization, this historic building stands once more dedicated to the spirit of '76. It signifies to our society the first tangible result of the purposes for which we are instituted, and an obligation whose sacredness will inspire the many generations which will arise to fill our places in increasing numbers in the future. It signifies to us, also, an unwritten bond of union between the people of Lebanon and ourselves, all the more effective for being unwritten, because it is made in the spirit of patriotism which we recognize in each other, and which alone can give force and permanence to such a bond.

It is, I am told, often lamented that, some forty years ago, the railroads were kept at a respectful distance from the heart of your town. The loss in growth, and in the development of the new and ugly, which may have resulted from this circumstance, is now requited by the fact that you can show to the Sons of the Revolution and to your other guests to-day, a town so little altered from the Lebanon of 1776, when the sessions of the Council of Safety in the War Office made it the delegated capital of our State. It is appropriate, too, that the American of the present day, and of future days, should undertake something which may savor to him of a pilgrimage when he pays his reverence at the shrine of the old War Office, though the journey would have appeared to his ancestors more than luxurious. The pride which you naturally feel in Lebanon's cradle of liberty will be fostered by the fact that, for this same reason, we must, to a great extent, delegate to you the care and custody of the building, uniting with you in plans which shall make it useful and attractive for the future.

Thanks to the honest carpentry of our ancestors, and thanks to the durability of our good old Connecticut oak, emblematic of patriotism, the old War Office, restored and repaired, will now last through many generations to come, inspiring our children and our children's children as it inspires us on this anniversary of the adoption of our country's flag.

At the conclusion of this address, Mr. Erastus Geer of Lebanon arose and introduced a most interesting feature in the exercises, which had not been placed upon the programme. Upon front seats on the platform were four venerable citizens of Lebanon. Mr. Geer introduced them to the large assemblage in the following words:

Mr. President, Sons, Assembly:

The War Office is the object of interest that calls us together to-day; but there is another feature of interest that is worthy of notice.

We have four citizens of Lebanon who are sons direct of Revolutionary soldiers. With pleasure we introduce them.

Colonel Anson Fowler, eighty-seven and a half years old, son of Amos Fowler, a revolutionary soldier who served in the war from beginning to end, was orderly sergeant; was in the battle at Long Island, and at Yorktown, and for a time was one of the twelve that composed General Washington's Life Guard. He had five brothers in the war, making six soldiers from one family. It is no surprise that Cornwallis surrendered.

It was John Fowler who bore the lamented Warren from the field at Bunker Hill. While doing it, a comrade came to his assistance, but John says, "No, I can do it; go and fight as hard as you can."

Colonel Fowler was the youngest of a family of twelve children, and is the only survivor. His military career was in the cavalry. He retired with the rank of Colonel. He tells us, that a few days since, he witnessed a lively sham fight on the field where his father fought on Long Island.

(Here, Colonel Fowler said he wished to say a word, and rising with a fifty-dollar note of old continental money in his hand, he said, holding the note to the view of the audience: "My father fought for eight dollars a month, and was paid in such stuff as this. When he returned from the war, with four fifty-dollar notes in his pocket, he could not buy a mug of flip with all of them." This speech elicited a hearty laugh from the audience.)

Mr. Geer, resuming, then said, I next introduce John D. Kingsley, eighty-three years old, the son of Ashael Kingsley, who entered the Revolutionary service in 1780, and afterwards became captain. Mr. Kingsley is the youngest of a family of six children, and is the only survivor.

I now introduce Deacon John D. Avery, eighty-four and a half years old, son of David Avery, who entered the service at the age of sixteen, at New London, soon after the Groton massacre. He afterwards became captain. Deacon Avery is the ninth of a family of ten children, and is the only survivor. His military service was that of a musician in the Flank Company, and a good soldier in the Baptist Church, fighting the good fight, and will win the crown.

Last I introduce Captain Griswold E. Morgan, eighty years old, son of William Avery Morgan, who was at Bunker Hill and at the battle of Long Island, where a British bullet passed through his hat — first through the brim where it was turned up *in front*, then through the crown, cutting a lock of hair from his head. He was orderly sergeant, and after the war became captain.

Captain Morgan is the sixteenth of a family of seventeen children, and is the only survivor. His military service was in the Lebanon militia, retiring as captain. He gave two sons, William E. and George H., to save the Union in the War of the Rebellion. The former received a ball in his arm, destroying the action of the elbow joint, and the latter died of fever in the hospital at Beaufort, N. C. The late Governor Morgan of New York was Captain Morgan's nephew, and Governor Morgan G. Bulkeley his great-great-nephew.

Honored Sons: We thank you for your presence with us to-day. We look upon you not as relics, but as treasures of your generation, which is the only direct link connecting us with the Revolution. Your fathers, our grandfathers, fought for and won the freedom which has made it possible for this country to become what it is to-day, the nation of nations. You have witnessed its growth from the thirteen original States clustered upon the Atlantic; it has increased in numbers arithmetically and in expanse geometrically. Stars have lit upon its flag like snowflakes.

(Applause.)

The President: Lebanon has done much for us to-day. She has given us the War Office, and has ably assisted us in honoring it, and she has loaned us four honored sons of Revolutionary sires. It is hardly a fitting time for us to ask more, but allow me to say to you, Mr. Geer, as a member of our Society, that Lebanon should give us these sons, as she has given us the War Office. (*Col-*

onel *Fowler:* "I am ready.") We will take them on the same terms, repairs and all, for they are specimens of our good old Connecticut oak, which needs no repairs. The only conveyance necessary is the filling up of that brief statement of pedigree and ancestor's service contained in our form of application for membership, with which you can provide them.

One of our poets has said, "Let me make my nation's songs, and I care not who makes its laws." We are happy in having among the contributors to this occasion one whose muse has often inspired the sentiment of patriotism, which makes lawgiving a matter of unused form. I have the honor and pleasure to announce a poem by Mr. Thomas S. Collier of New London.

Mr. Collier read the following poem, which he had kindly composed for the occasion:

POEM BY MR. THOMAS S. COLLIER.

What is the soul of a nation?
  Lo, is it not deeds well done?
Red blood poured out as libation?
  Hard toil till the end is won?
Swift blows, when the smoke goes drifting
  From the cannon, hot with flame?
And work, when the war clouds, lifting,
  Show the blazoning of fame?
These hold that affluence golden,
  Bright fire of sword and pen,
Which from the ages olden
  Has thrilled the hearts of men.

Not where the trumpets bluster,
  And answering bugles sound,
As martial legions muster,
  Are all the heroes found;
But where the orchards blooming
  Foams white the hills along,
And bees, with lazy booming,
  Wake the brown sparrow's song,

By quiet hearths are beating
   The hearts that watch and wait,
With thought each act completing,
   That conquers Time and Fate;
Rounding with patient labor
   The work of those who died,
Where sabre clashed with sabre
   Above war's sanguine tide.

Here was no field of battle,
   These hills no echoes gave
Of that fierce rush and rattle
   Whose harvest is the grave;
Yet where the drums were calling,
   And where the fight was hot,
And men were swiftly falling
   Before the whistling shot,
No soul with hope was stronger
   Than that which blossomed here—
No voice, as days grew longer,
   Was louder with its cheer.

Ah, souls were bent and shaken
   As days grew into years,
And saw no bright hope waken
   To gleam amid the tears—
Heard no call, triumph sounding,
   From mountain side and gorge,
Only the low graves rounding—
   The gloom of Valley Forge;
Yet here a strength unbroken
   Met all the storm-filled days,
Rising sublime, a token
   Of faith, in weary ways.

What built the power, unfolding
   Such glorious purpose, when
War's carnival was holding
   High feast with homes and men?

When grew the thought, whose glory
  Burned like a sun supreme,
Above the fields, all gory
  With battle's crimson stream?
Where bloomed the manhood, keeping
  Such steadfast step and strong,
When the red sword was reaping
  The harvesting of wrong?
Here in the peace, and tender
  Warm light of heart and hearth,
Was born that virile splendor
  Which filled the waiting earth, —
That flame of Freedom, rising
  In broadening waves of light,
The souls of men surprising,
  And lifting them from night;
Here, and in kindred places,
  The fire that all could see
Shone from determined faces,
  And taught men to be free.

Why are we gathered together?
  The land is full of peace,
And high in the halcyon weather
  The songs of labor increase.
What makes the drums beat, ringing
  Their challenge to the hills?
Why are the bugles flinging
  Swift calls to marts and mills?
Because these walls have cherished
  A memory bright and high;
No name they knew has perished,
  For deeds can never die;
And here, when hearts were beating,
  Half hoping, half in fear,
Strong souls, in council meeting,
  Spoke firm, and loud, and clear.

There was no weak denying.
  There was no backward glance,
But where the flags were flying,
  And red shone sword and lance.
Their words rang swift and cheerful,
  And skies grew bright again,
For those whose hearts were fearful,
  For these were master men;
And one led, who unknowing
  Linked to the land his name,
By earnest manhood showing
  How near we live to fame.

Ours is the sunlit morning —
  Ours is the noontide's gold
And the radiant light adorning
  The paths once dark and cold;
But the savor of our treasure
  Was the salt of toil, and tears,
And want, that filled the measure
  Of long and bitter years;
We drink the wine of gladness,
  We reap the harvest sheaves,
Whose seed was sown in sadness,
  And the drift of yellow leaves;
With faith, and not with grieving,
  Was built the mighty past;
What good gift are we leaving
  To those who follow fast?
What thought, what deed, what glory
  Shall mark this epoch ours,
And leave our names and story
  High set where grandeur towers?

What thing shall make men cherish
  The memory of to-day?
Ah, actions will not perish
  Though monuments decay.

We see, spread out before us,
    The fairest land of earth,
Loud with the ringing chorus
    That only here has birth;
Ours is the holy duty
    To build, with firmer hand,
This heritage of beauty,
    That it may ever stand;
Our deeds should make more lasting
    The freedom that has grown
From toil, and tears, and fasting,
    And strength of blood and bone.
Then like the blossoms vernal
    That with the spring combine,
Our age will shine eternal,
    To all mankind a sign;
A star serene, yet showing
    Near kindred to the sun,
Whereon these names are glowing —
    Trumbull and Washington.

(Applause.)

The President: The transition from poetry to prose is usually abrupt and depressing; but we are fortunately so situated to-day that, in making this transition, we shall only pass from one inspiration to another. No one could more fittingly deliver the address now to follow than one of Lebanon ancestry whose utterances from the rostrum and through the press have marked him as the champion of the things honest, true, and of good report, of which the apostle speaks.

I take great pride and pleasure in announcing an address by the Reverend Dr. Leonard W. Bacon, the orator of the day.

Dr. Bacon spoke as follows:

MR. BACON'S ADDRESS.

It is written in an ancient report of an old-time oration on some public occasion in New England, that the orator began by *disabling himself*. It was only a phrase of the English of the period, to signify that the speaker began by acknowledging his disqualifications for the function he was about to attempt — a most injudicious form of exordium, which has not gone wholly out of fashion to this day. Let the audience find out for themselves, if they can, that the speaker is not master of his subject; if they do not find it out, why should he be so foolish as to tell them?

Do not expect from me, then, any superfluous acknowledgments of what is perfectly understood between us already. It was only after those had declined, to whom the thoughts of all had naturally turned as the fitting and representative spokesmen for this occasion and this venerable place, that the committee had recourse, at a late hour, to one whose fitness consists in his bearing, by inheritance, the name of a most loving, learned, and eloquent historian of the best and noblest things in the past of New England and especially of Connecticut; and in his being at two removes a son of this ancient town of Lebanon. Whether also a Son of the Revolution by virtue of any deeds in arms of the Beaumonts and the Parks of this town he cannot say, having been too much occupied in caring for his descendants to pay, as yet, much attention to his ancestors. Such qualifications, joined with a true and reverent love for the occasion and the subject, are my only fitness for this office. I can hope to make no contribution to the rich stores of history that have been already gathered; but only to revive your own memories of the great and heroic history that centered in the old War Office, and in the person of Governor Jonathan Trumbull the First, and to reiterate the lessons of patriotic virtue that it teaches, lessons that cannot be heard too often nor too deeply impressed.

At the very threshold of our study of the subject, we need to divest our minds of the false impression conveyed by the current popular name of the War of Independence. In others of the thirteen colonies, this war was indeed a "Revolutionary War." But Connecticut never had a revolutionary war. Let other States recount the blessings that have accrued to them as the results of the Revolution, and the cost in blood and treasure that was paid for them, saying, as well they may, "with a great price obtained I this freedom." But let Connecticut never forget to make her proud reply, "but I was freeborn." The commonwealths of Virginia and Massachusetts were first, perhaps, to feel the irksomeness and galling of the yoke of bondage. The free democratic republic of Connecticut, free, democratic, and independent from its first inception, never ceased to be free and independent except in name. The people whose "strong bent of mind" inclined them to seek a settlement outside the chartered limits of any existing colony — they and their children were a chosen people who never were in bondage to any man. The history of that wonderful prophetic constitution of Connecticut first told in monograph by my father,* since illuminated by the research of Dr. Hammond Trumbull, now known and honored by the first publicists of the world, as for instance by Dr. Bryce in his classic volumes on the American Commonwealth, has just now been admirably retold by Mr. Alexander Johnston † and by Mr. Joseph H. Twichell.‡ We all know now, thanks to these lucid exponents, what unique glory in the history of Civil Liberty belongs to "Mr. Hooker's company" and pre-eminently to that divinely anointed prophet of the coming age, Thomas Hooker himself. We know that it was on the banks of the Connecticut, 250 years ago, that the first notes of that march were

---

*Discourse on the early Constitutional History of Connecticut, delivered before the Connecticut Historical Society, Hartford, May 17, 1843, by Leonard Bacon. Hartford, 1843. pp. 24.

†"Connecticut" in the American Commonwealth Series.

‡Historical address delivered at Hartford January 24, 1889, and published by the Connecticut Historical Society.

sounded to which the constitutional liberties of America and the world are keeping time to-day. And the next chapter in the history is no less marvelous than the first, the chapter which tells how, when the first of all written constitutions had to be superseded by a royal charter, the work of Hooker, Haynes, and Ludlow and the people whom they led was so conserved by "the accomplished diplomacy of the younger Winthrop," that the change from constitution to charter was practically little more than a change of name. The original free democratic republic went on as before, choosing its own governors and legislators, enacting and enforcing its own laws. No royal assent was ever asked or given to a Connecticut statute. No royal governor ever successfully asserted his authority on Connecticut soil. Among the "Sons of the Revolution" the Connecticut society is entitled to a pre-eminence as sons of sires who were always free, and who fought in a war which was for them no revolution, not to win freedom for themselves, but to win it for other commonwealths less privileged, and for themselves to maintain it always inviolate, under a title, not of human rights, but of a divine right not less sacred and far better attested than any *jus divinum* ever pretended by Stuart or Hanoverian.

Naturally, this characteristic of the War of Independence in Connecticut, that it was a war, not of revolution, but of conservation, gave a characteristic steady and conservative tone to the course of the State throughout the war. Elsewhere the war was a rebellion, the insurgent people arming against the constituted government. Here, it was the State itself, as an organic unit, under its constitutional and lawful officers, arming in its own defense against a threat of revolution to be enforced upon it from without. And it moved with calmness, dignity, and solid weight. There was no need here of the stormy eloquence which rocked the Cradle of Liberty, and stirred up the stones of Boston streets to mutiny. There was no occasion, there was no chance, for fights like Lexington and Concord and Bunker Hill. The people and the State were one. There was no domestic enemy. There were individual tories — and an unhappy time they had of it — but there was no tory party. There was no hospitality here for invading armies. Never but twice did they venture to stay over night, and never did they wait long enough to be whipped. Therefore it is that we are so poor in battlefields and in monuments of that period. What fighting Connecticut had to do — and she did her full share — had to be done on the soil of other States.

I do not know the particular origin of that *sobriquet* which characterizes our State as "the land of steady habits." But it may well have had its rise in the sobriety and tenacity with which Connecticut so sovereignly moved into the war and then moved on with it. I have already given reasons why it could not be so with the neighbor States. The Scripture saith not in vain, "Oppression maketh a wise man mad." There were wise men in the Bay State, and when actual oppression began, they were mad, very mad indeed. Massachusetts had more than once asserted her claim to the hegemony among the New England colonies, and at this time was much disposed to force the fighting; was much vexed indeed, when Connecticut, instead of falling promptly into line behind her Committees of Safety, continued in correspondence through her Governor with the royal Governor Gage at Boston, as between co-ordinate authorities, seeking in all sincerity to avert the war for which nevertheless she went on making strenuous preparation. But Massachusetts patriots had reason to change their mind, and to be thankful for the sober, steady little State to the south of them which moved in solid organization beside them into the smoke and dust of the fight, never hurrying and never flinching. They came to think better of Connecticut when from all her towns the supplies voted regularly in her town meetings came flowing in to the relief of beleaguered Boston, and especially when the thirty barrels of gunpowder that had been stored by provident Governor Jonathan Trumbull arrived in time to fill the cartridge-boxes and the powder-horns on Bunker Hill.

Great as was the advantage to the cause of America and freedom in the existence of a State like Connecticut, not disorganized by the war, these advantages would have been nullified, or worse, if the head of the State had been feeble and timid like Governor Wanton of Rhode Island, or a bitter and malignant tory like Trumbull's Harvard classmate, Governor Hutchinson of Massachusetts. What was needed was a wise, energetic, patriotic governor at the head of a patriotic State. And it was to meet this exigency that God raised up Jonathan Trumbull, and trained him with a singularly varied discipline for a great career. It was wisely fitted to the time and the place that this training should begin with the college education which in early New England, before the days of professional seminaries, was eminently a theological education, fitting one for the ministry of the gospel, and in a State whose system of laws was distinctly and professedly founded on the Institutes of Moses, fitting one no less for the profession of the law and for all the relations of civil and political life. It was a noble and worthy beginning of life, to begin with the diligent and enthusiastic study of the Scriptures in Greek and Hebrew, and with the religious purpose of devoting his life to the ministry of Jesus Christ. But for a more special preparation for his destined work, the wit of man could have invented nothing more exactly fitting than that into which he was presently coerced by providential circumstances — the business of a country merchant as it was then carried on. How completely and marvelously different from our conditions were those in which a great and far-reaching mercantile business, spreading into all parts of the State and into other States and sailing its own ships for export and import into distant seas of either hemisphere, could grow up having its principal headquarters in an inland farming town, is a subject on which we all know something, but on which we might all be glad to be taught by some such master of economic history as David A. Wells. But the essential fact is clear, that the country-store of Trumble, Fitch & Trumble brought its proprietors into practical acquaintance with all the resources of the country and their relations to the trade of the world. Presently his position as Colonel of a regiment of Connecticut militia in those French and Indian wars that were the West Point in which our Revolutionary officers were trained, gave him occasion to study the application of the country's resources to the uses of war. Meanwhile the good, old-fashioned steady habit, before "rotation in office" had been invented, of keeping a good officer in the public service when once his qualities had been proved, was exercising Trumbull successively in legislative and judicial functions; for successive years he held the seat of chief-justice of the Commonwealth. His education was becoming complete. He became Governor of Connecticut just as the years of trial were drawing nigh that were to put to illustrious use for the salvation of the whole American nation, all his judicial wisdom, and all his executive sagacity and energy.

It is easy for us to read a providential purpose in those ill winds which swept from the sea all his ships in a single year, and brought his firm to bankruptcy. They released his time and strength from private cares, that they might be given wholly to the service of the imperilled country; and they vacated the old country-store of its merchandise, that it might become, practically, and some of the time literally, the headquarters of the commissary department of the United States during the War of Independence.

Let me not attempt to tell of the doings under the roof of the old War Office. They ought, indeed, to be told as they never have been. Whoever shall write the history of the recruiting and the commissariat of the Continental army, will tell the story, not of the most showy, but, I do not hesitate to say, of the most arduous, part of the War of Independence. When it came to this anxious and perplexing work, the national leaders were glad to bethink them of the State which had no fiery popular orator, a Sam Adams or a Patrick Henry, to kindle the general patriotism, because it had no function for him; which had no record of stormy uprisings or domestic conflicts, because its people were all of one mind; which had no petty vice-regal court to be a center of tainting influence and anti-patriotic intrigue; which had no battle-fields to show, because its soil was so intolerant of hostile feet — the State which free from internal dissension and from hostile occupation had, as no other had, both the power and the will to give its entire resources of men and material to the general good. This, no doubt, determined the appointment to the office of Commissary-General of the Continental Army, of Governor Trumbull's eldest son Joseph, a man like-minded with his father; and when he sank under its exhausting labors and crushing responsibilities, as truly a martyr to American freedom as Warren on the field or Nathan Hale on the scaffold, the same reason called for the appointment of another Connecticut man as his successor, Col. Wadsworth, and required him to come from Hartford and fix his headquarters here hard by the Governor's house and office in Lebanon.

One may read in Stuart's Life of Trumbull something of the details of the business that was done in the old War Office — the ceaseless and tireless meetings of the Committee of Safety — the coming and going of couriers with dispatches to and from Congress and the generals and the Commander-in-chief — the fitting-out of provision-trains and supplies of beef upon the hoof — the raising of recruits for the dwindling army — the ordering of militia regiments to threatened points of the State frontier, and to the relief of neighbor States — the equipping and commissioning and commanding of Connecticut's adventurous little navy — the councils of war and of state there held with Washington and other Continental generals, with Rochambeau and the Duke de Lauzun and other French commanders, military and naval. One may read of them there, and in some other special and local histories, but not, I am bound to say it, in any just or due proportion, in the general histories of the war. The latest of these, by John Fiske, a great man, Connecticut-born, a man who knows the difference between surface and substance, between the pomp and circumstance of war and the hard, steady work of it, and who is aware that an army, like a serpent, moves on its belly, tells the story of the American Revolution in two volumes, and (I am informed) dispatches the part done by Jonathan Trumbull in twelve words.

The time came, in the course of the struggle, when it might have been pardoned to the infirmity of human nature if the doubt had occurred to some of the sons of Connecticut whether the magnificent unselfishness of her course had not been overdone. That was the time when the British war policy changed from one of hope, of conciliation mingled with severity, to a policy of desperation and destruction and ravage. No wonder that the State whose sons were found in arms everywhere but on their own soil, whose hard-tilled acres furnished so largely the subsistence and whose mines and mills furnished the equipment of the Continental forces, should be the first and favorite quarry for British vengeance. It was then that Norwalk and Fairfield and New Haven went up in smoke, and at last, when, after counseling with Washington over the plan of the Yorktown campaign, the French troops that had been cantoned in Lebanon and elsewhere, with all that Connecticut could spare, and more, of her last remaining forces, had been sent far south for the final struggle of the war, — it was then that the fleet bearing "traitor Arnold and his murthering crew"* crept through the Sound on its mis-

---

* The phrase of righteous horror and detestation that is inscribed on scores of head-stones in various cemeteries of Southeastern Connecticut, over graves of victims of the Groton massacre.

sion of destruction and massacre at New London and Groton.

> The Governor's face grew sad,
>   In his store on Lebanon hill;
> He reckoned the men he had;
>   He counted the forts to fill;
> He traced on the map the ground
>   By river, and harbor, and coast,—
> " Ah, where shall the men and the guns be found,
>   Lest the State be lost?"
>
> The brave State's sons were gone;
>   On many a field they lay;
> They were following Washington,
>   Afar down Yorktown way;
> The men and the weapons failed,
>   They were gone with our free good-will;
> But Jonathan Trumbull never quailed,
>   In his store on Lebanon hill.
>
> There was New London fort,
>   And the fort on Groton Height,
> And the rich and crowded port;
>   But where were the men to fight?
> Might it not be we had erred
>   To care for our homes so ill?
> Nay, never a word of such grudge was heard
>   On Lebanon hill.
>
> Remember, citizens, and
>   If ever the ill thought comes
> To reck less of the broad, great land,
>   And more of your own small homes,
> Think of your fathers' dust;
>   Think of their brave good-will,
> And the Puritan Governor's toil and trust
>   On Lebanon hill.*

If there were time, and the question were not rather what to omit than what to say, it would be a most interesting matter to take this figure of Jonathan Trumbull, the finest and most perfect type of the Puritan magistrate of the eighteenth century, and study it in

---

* From a poem recited at Groton, on the one hundredth anniversary of the massacre, September 8, 1881.

comparison and contrast with other typical men with whom he was closely associated.

One would have been more struck with the points of likeness than of difference between Trumbull, son of the New England Puritans, and Washington, son of the Virginian Cavaliers, as they met for the first time at Colonel Huntington's house in Norwich.

But if it is true (I find no evidence or probability of it) that the Governor once entertained Thomas Jefferson in this venerable and hospitable mansion, it must have been by a supreme effort of courtesy and policy on both sides that the irreconcilable contrariety between the theologian-governor and the free-thinking political *doctrinaire* of the French school was kept from breaking out openly — as it did indeed break out in sharp words, on a later occasion, between Jefferson and the governor's son John, the painter, a man who rarely erred by excess of meekness.* The difference is most vividly illustrated in two memorable papers — Jefferson's Declaration of Independence of July 4, 1776, and that solemn proclamation of Governor Trumbull of twenty days earlier, lately discovered by the keen eye of Mr. Hoadly, and characterized, perhaps with a strained use of the word, as "the Connecticut Declaration of Independence."† The one starts with an enumeration of self-evident truths, and with a doctrine of human rights, and is grounded on the principles of the *contrat social* of Jean Jacques Rousseau. The other begins with the creation and the fall of man, is grounded on the Holy Scriptures, and is the utterance throughout of a lofty and noble religious faith. Jefferson's Declaration, accepted as the voice of the American people, is famous through the world. The proclamation of Trumbull has only just now been rescued from its century of oblivion by the hand of the patient antiquary. But we may

---

* The incident is told by Colonel John in his interesting volume of Reminiscences, p. 171.

† See Appendix, p. 83.

safely challenge the twentieth century to pronounce between the two as to which is the nobler, more solemnly eloquent document, and the worthier of the great theme which is common to them both.

A contrast even more antagonistic would be that between Trumbull and the faded-out, apostate Puritanism embodied in that brilliant soldier from the next-neighbor town, who seemed also at first to be a great and generous patriot, Benedict Arnold. What was the estimate of Arnold, from the beginning, on the part of his own native State and its governor, is seen in the fact that they constantly refused to trust him. He never bore a Connecticut commission. His titles and honors and his opportunities of treason all came to him from other States, or from the continental authorities. It is to the honor of his native State that she rejected him, and that he hated her in return with a malignant hatred.

But a contrast as startling and intense as the canvas of history has ever exhibited was that which was exhibited here on Lebanon green when the French regiments lay cantoned here in winter quarters. Where, in American history at least, could such subjects be found for romance, or for the pencil of the historical painter? These representatives of the gayest, most brilliant, most corrupt and vicious court in Europe, what kind of figure did they make in the midst of the severe simplicity of old Lebanon? We are not without some record of their impressions, in the journal of the Count de Rochambeau and the travels of the Marquis de Chastellux. But the contrast between the foremost personage among the Frenchmen here, the gay Duke de Lauzun, who made his headquarters at the house of David Trumbull, and the serious, precise figure of the governor is drawn already to our hand by the graceful pencil of Donald Mitchell.

"And what a contrast it is — this gay nobleman, carved out, as it were, from the dissolute age of Louis XV., who had sauntered under the colonnades of the

Trianon, and had kissed the hand of the Pompadour, now strutting among the staid dames of Norwich and of Lebanon! How they must have looked at him and his fine troopers from under their knitted hoods! You know, I suppose, his after history; how he went back to Paris, and among the wits there was wont to mimic the way in which the stiff old Connecticut governor had said grace at his table. Ah! he did not know that in Governor Trumbull, and all such men, is the material to found an enduring state; and in himself, and all such men, only the inflammable material to burn one down. There is a life written of Governor Trumbull, and there is a life written of the Marquis [duke] of Lauzun. The first is full of deeds of quiet heroism, ending with a tranquil and triumphant death; the other is full of the rankest gallantries, and ends with a little spurt of blood under the knife of the guillotine upon the gay Place de la Concorde." *

This is an occasion when the orator cannot comfort himself with the rhetorical maxim that "no one knows the good things that you leave out," for every one knows them, and judges the speaker for his sins of omission. We cannot say all that ought to be said, but we must not stop at such a point as to leave the impression that "the glory of Lebanon" ceased when that stately cedar fell — the first Governor Trumbull. There was a goodly forest of Lebanon in other names beside that of Trumbull. But in that one stock the names of the second governor and the third governor show the divine law of heredity working with the promise of the divine covenant to children's children; and show this democratic people, so ready to prune off and fling into the Gehenna-heap any degenerate scion, even of the noblest parentage, that sinks himself down to general worthlessness and *baccarat*, are not ungenerous, as other names, like Winthrop and Adams and Harrison, have proved, to honor ancestral virtues fitly worn by worthy

---

* Speech at the Norwich Jubilee, 1859.

sons. And this day reminds us that if Connecticut should seek in the old stock for the old style of Christian probity and faithful citizenship with which to dignify her list of worthies by adding to it the title of a new Brother Jonathan, a Governor Trumbull the Fourth, she need not seek in vain.

There is another line of pedigree, too, down which the influence of the great names and examples of the Lebanon heroes has descended. It is a line not always as easy to be traced as that of natural genealogy, but it is sometimes clear enough. There is the story, for instance, of the country boy who grew up in this old town some fourscore years ago, where, in the vast amplitude of the town street, he marked the traces of the old French camp, and where every house was inhabited with heroic memories and traditions. I love to imagine the handsome little fellow wandering thoughtfully among the gravestones in the old burying-ground, that tell of holy ministers, and brave soldiers, and upright citizens, and pausing to read the four inscriptions on the Trumbull monument, recording the career of one who, by the force and dignity of his character, rose from private station to be the foremost man in all the commonwealth, and, next to Washington himself, the chief promoter of his country's liberty. I love to imagine how that shining example of a Christian patriot dwelt in the young man's mind when he had removed from ancestral Lebanon to Norwich for the beginning of his fair career; and how, in the midst of daily duties in counting-room and church and municipal business, the lineaments of that heroic Puritan character unconsciously reproduced themselves in his mind; and as great events went on, and lifted him as by a rising tide into the highest station in the State, history for once consented to repeat itself, and to complete that impressive parallel on which later historians of Connecticut will delight to dwell, between the great War Governor of the War for Independence, and the great War Governor of the War for the Union and the Constitution.

We want to see the bright succession perpetuated along *this* line of descent to all generations. Let this be a result of our gathering here to-day to hoist the old flag again over the old War Office now secured by the patriotic gift of its venerable owner as a lasting monument of the great deeds it has witnessed. Let it not be said that the fair and fertile acres of this ancient township have lost their old quality and become sterile of great men. To this end, citizens of Lebanon, let not this stir of patriotic feeling end with the jubilation of to-day. Let it enter into the education of your children. Let it be settled that in your common schools the study of American history begins with the history of Lebanon, the object-lessons of which are about them on every side. Let the great families sprung from this soil, but all removed from it without leaving a representative behind them — the se-cedars of Lebanon, as they might be called — families illustrated everywhere in the land except here, in the highest stations of church and state — be called upon to "remember the hole of the pit whence they were digged," and to provide liberally that the great deeds here enacted by the sires shall be so worthily commemorated as to reflect honor instead of discredit on the scattered descendants. Let it be their task — it is not conceivable that they should decline it — to provide that the old burying-ground where their fathers lie, instead of being, as now, with its tumbling monuments and overgrown epitaphs, a very emblem of neglect and sheer oblivion, shall show the proofs of pious and reverent care. It will do them good, as well as you and your children. But the best of the work and of its fruits will be with you of the Lebanon of to-day, to whose faithful custody this sacred charge of the graves of saints and heroes is of necessity personally committed.

> "Guard well your trust,
> The truth that made them free,
> The faith that dared the sea,
> Their cherished purity,
> Their garnered dust."

The President: This occasion has been honored by many expressions from invited guests, some of whom have sent to us expressions of interest and of patriotic sentiment which should be heard now. I will ask our vice-president, the Hon. E. J. Hill, to read such extracts from these letters as we have been able to select for the limited time which we can devote to that purpose.

The Vice-President: I will first read a letter from the Hon. Levi P. Morton, Vice-President of the United States:

"RHINECLIFF, N. Y., June 9, 1891.

"DEAR SIR: I regret very much that a previous engagement makes it impossible for me to accept your kind invitation to be present on the occasion of the transfer of the Lebanon War Office to your Society, and the commemoration of the adoption of our National flag. The event is one in which I take much interest, and would much like to attend.

"Very truly yours, L. P. MORTON."

The Minister of France writes:

"I beg to assure you that I sincerely appreciate the thought which has prompted your kind invitation, and in reply, to express my regret that a previous engagement will prevent me from being in your midst next week.

"Respectfully yours, TH. ROUSTAN,
French Minister."

The Hon. Thomas F. Bayard, ex-Secretary of State:

"I regret that engagements already made will prevent my leaving home on the day appointed (the 15th inst.). I should have felt deep interest in the locality of your meeting, and the object."

The Hon. William Wirt Henry:

"I congratulate the Connecticut Society on its auspicious beginning, and trust it may be a potent agent in keeping fresh the memories of our glorious Revolution."

Mr. Frederick S. Tallmadge, President of the New York Society of Sons of the Revolution:
"So long as our Societies live and prosper under the protection of the flag with thirteen stars, so long our pride and patriotism will know no bounds."

Mr. Paul Revere of the New Jersey Society:
"Permit me to congratulate you on your acquiring so interesting a memorial of the Revolution, and to wish you every pleasure in celebrating its acquirement and the anniversary of the adoption of our national flag."

Hon. Lyman Trumbull of Chicago:
"I am much gratified to witness the renewed interest which, of late years, seems to be taken by the present generation in tracing their origin back to the heroes of the Revolution, and in commemorating the important events of that most interesting period in our country's history. It serves to keep alive that spirit of patriotism which animated our forefathers in securing our independence as a nation, and establishing a government based upon the liberty and equality of all its inhabitants."

The Rev. Dr. Edward Everett Hale:
"The occasion interests me much, and there is no place which I wish to see more. I take great interest in the Sons of the Revolution. I am theoretically connected with them here, but know a great deal more of their work at the West. There, their men have been the central men in what I call the education for patriotism,— a thing vastly important there or here."

Mr. William G. Hamilton of New York:
"Knowing how well your Society will care for and preserve this historic building, which so nobly links the

past with the present, this event will have a most salutary effect in re-arousing patriotic sentiments, and do much good to the cause of the Sons of the Revolution."

Hon. Champion S. Chase, Omaha, Neb.:
"Here's to Connecticut, a State whose patriotic sons do not forget to celebrate the victories of her fathers, achieved on many a battlefield, when America was first saved for Americans."

A telegram received to-day from Mr. John W. Buchanan, Secretary of the Kentucky Society:
"Sons of the American Revolution of Kentucky greet you and give three cheers for the flag with thirteen stars. We are as heartily with you to-day as were our forefathers with yours an hundred years ago, when they

'Their flag to April's breeze unfurled,
And fired the shot heard round the world.'"

Dr. Daniel C. Gilman, President of the Johns Hopkins University, and a member of the Connecticut Society, writes:
"If I were free, it would give me the greatest pleasure to accept the invitation for June 15th, but I am detained here by the fact that our session closes on that very day, and it would be quite unworthy for a Son of the Revolution to be absent from his post at the time of an important engagement."

A telegram from the Hon. William D. Cabell of Washington:
"Heartfelt congratulations! The Sons of the District rejoice with you."

A telegram from Mr. J. C. Pampelly of the New Jersey Society:
"Present this sentiment: Our national flag. May its red, white, and blue be to the Sons a perpetual incite-

ment to courage of conviction, purity of purpose, and unswerving vigilance."

Hon. Edwin S. Barrett, President of the Massachusetts Society, writes:
"Connecticut, ever the ally of Massachusetts in the Revolution, is kindly remembered when she celebrates her historic events."

Hon. Nathanael Greene, President of the Rhode Island Society of the Cincinnati:
"You have my best wishes that the occasion may be an enjoyable one, and that it may help to preserve in the memory of the American people the inestimable privileges we inherit from our illustrious fathers of the Revolution."

Hon. Albert Edgerton, President of the Minnesota Society, S. A. R.:
"I am rejoiced that an old landmark around which cluster such interesting memories of events of mighty importance, is to become the property of your Society, to be sacredly guarded, and kept as a beacon light for posterity."

The Rev. Dr. John P. Gulliver of Andover, Mass.:
"I can only express to you personally my high appreciation of the work your Society has undertaken in regard to the memorabilia of the Revolutionary period. Any service, however trivial, which this generation can render, will increase in value as the years roll on."

The Right Reverend Frederick D. Huntington of Syracuse, New York:
"From my father and resident relatives I have almost all my life been receiving information about the history and inhabitants of Lebanon, both orally and in writing, and I have come to feel an attachment for its soil and scenery."

Letters of regret had also been received from Hon.
Redfield Proctor, Secretary of War, President Charles
W. Eliot of Harvard, Dr. William Seward Webb, President-General of the National Society S. A. R., Major
Asa Bird Gardiner, Secretary-General of the Society of
the Cincinnati, Mrs. Flora Adams Darling of the Daughters of the Revolution, General Alexander S. Webb, Mr.
Charles H. Woodruff, General William S. Stryker,
President E. B. Andrews of Brown University, Dr.
Henry A. Coit of St. Paul's School, Mr. Richard M. Cadwalader, President of the Pennsylvania Society S. R.,
General William B. Franklin, Hon. John Whitehead,
President of the New Jersey Society S. A. R., Mr. Frederick Van Lennep of New York, Mr. James M. Montgomery, Mr. Clarence W. Bowen, Mr. R. Fulton Ludlow,
Mr. Henry E. Turner, Vice-President of the Rhode
Island Cincinnati, Mr. G. Washington Ball, nearest
lineal male descendant of George Washington, President
Timothy Dwight of Yale, Mr. Luther L. Tarbell, and
the Hon. William H. Arnoux.

After the celebration, letters were received from Ex-President Grover Cleveland, Ex-Minister Edward J.
Phelps, and the Right Reverend Charles E. Cheney, all
of whom, owing to absence from home, were unable to
reply to their invitations at the time of their receipt.
These letters all express deep interest in the occasion,
and full sympathy with its objects.

At the conclusion of the reading of the letters, the
President called upon the Hon. Charles A. Russell,
Member of Congress for the Third Connecticut District,
in which the town of Lebanon and the War Office
are located. After repeated calls from the audience, Mr.
Russell appeared at the front of the platform, declining
to make a formal address, and greeting the audience
substantially as follows:

ADDRESS OF HON. CHARLES A. RUSSELL.

Mr. President, Sons of the American Revolution, Kind Friends of Lebanon:

It was my expectation to attest interest and pleasure on this occasion by my presence rather than by my utterance. And at this closing hour of a most delightful day I am inclined to think that this splendid gathering has been sufficiently enthused by the glorious memorials of the past, and by the stirring eloquence of those who have already spoken. I judge that we all are about ready to join in singing with patriotic spirit, and with fervent thanksgiving, "Our Country, 'tis of thee," as a fitting close to the exercises of the day, and then to go home with the inspiration and the assurance of another century of prosperous nationality looming before us. At any rate, I am not disposed to extend the programme beyond the opportunity of offering greeting to all who have in any way planned and carried forward this object lesson of grand American history, and expressing satisfaction at the pleasant and perfect result of their work.

Yet I have one thought which I would briefly give to you. As I came on to this Lebanon common to-day a worthy citizen of the town said to me: "This is a day when we pick up the history of our old backwoods country towns in New England, and introduce history and town to the country." There was a world of meaning in that remark, and it struck me as mighty fortunate for the country to have such introduction now and then. I believe it well for the Republic at large to form acquaintance with the history and character of its "country towns." They are now, as in the past, the stiff backbone of the nation. They possess, in most unadulterated form, the sturdy character and reliable action of a free populace in a free country. They have never been wanting in all the trials of our nationality, and they have stood stolidly for good government and good citizenship. There can no great harm come to our beloved institutions and our fair land while these "country towns" preserve their pristine virtues, and continue to furnish true men and noble women from the farms to build up the firesides of homes all over the country. So I rejoice at this chance which introduces Lebanon in its history and present worth to the country. The nation will learn that it has not yet exhausted its rich deposit of loyal strength and patriotic progress on Lebanon hills. [Applause.]

And taking example from this occasion, and from the Connecticut Society of the Sons of the American Revolution, and from the good town of Lebanon, I hope for more and more such introductions of "country towns" to our general populace. And to the end that our children and youth may know the better of our history, and our citizenship may trust the better to its power, I urge a wider acquaintance with the character of the sturdy yeomanry of "the country town." This occasion has especially directed attention to the Lebanon patriots, and I look forward to the near future when nation or state shall erect suitable memorials at the tombs of Lebanon patriots. [Applause.]

The President: Twenty-nine years ago a bill was introduced in Congress, and eloquently advocated by a son of Connecticut, providing for the observance of the anniversary of the adoption of our national flag. In the stirring legislation of those troublous times of 1862 the bill was laid upon that convenient and capacious piece of congressional furniture, the table, and has there remained, badly "snowed under," ever since. Its champion, to whom I have referred, the Hon. Mr. Dwight Loomis, has honored us with his presence to-day. We had hoped that he could remain long enough to take the flag-day bill from the table on this occasion, but since he has been obliged to leave us, let me pass that duty to the originator of the movement, Mr. Jonathan F. Morris, whose untiring interest in the matter and whose earnest efforts in promoting the movement fit him peculiarly to speak on this subject.

Mr. Morris spoke as follows:

MR. JONATHAN F. MORRIS'S ADDRESS.

Ladies and Gentlemen, Sons of the American Revolution and Fellow Members of the Connecticut Historical Society:

I very much regret the absence of Judge Loomis, who was expected to address you on the topic on which I am called to speak, for he would have much better discharged this duty than I, especially in regard to the action of Congress twenty-nine years ago, to which President Trumbull has referred.

President Trumbull has introduced me as the originator of "Flag Day." I should be very proud indeed if I were entirely worthy of such distinction, for while it is true that I perhaps did make the first suggestion in regard to the observance of the day, I was not alone in bringing the matter to public attention.

I am asked to give you the history of "Flag Day," which originated just thirty years ago. Thirty years ago! How rapidly have the years sped away! What mighty changes have those thirty years wrought in the world's history! What changes in our own land! Thirty years ago the nation was in the first throes of a civil war. I need not recount to you the events of that war; they are still fresh in the memory of every one in middle life. I need only to recall to your recollection its early days. You remember the secession of several States from the Union; the rejection of the Constitution of the Republic and its authority by their inhabitants. You remember how the Stars and Stripes were pulled down, cast aside, and trodden in the dust as "a detested rag." You remember the beleaguered fortress in Charleston harbor, and its nearly starving garrison. You remember that dismal night and that eventful day, April 12, 1861, when, with the break of day, a shot was fired from a battery on James Island on the flag on Fort Sumter. You remember the exciting days which followed; the call to arms by President Lincoln; the rising of the people; the rallying of the troops for the defense of the Union; the spontaneous and universal raising of flags. How from mast and spire, from tower and turret, from private houses and public buildings, the flag was flung to the breeze. Never before in all its history had it been so displayed. Banners were everywhere.

> "Banners from balcony, banners from the steeple,
> Banners from house to house, draping the people;
> Banners upborne by all, men, women, and children,
> Banners on horses' fronts, flashing, bewildering."

Indeed, with the revival of patriotism there seemed a baptism of flags. In these exciting days the Union Army gathered on the banks of the Potomac, and before the end of May fifty thousand men were waiting and watching the foe which menaced Washington. Among the soldiers from Connecticut was Joseph R. Hawley, to whose patriotic address you have listened to-day. At the outbreak of the rebellion he was the editor of the *Hartford Evening Press*. On receiving the news of the President's call for troops, he dropped his pen, and leaving his paper in the hands of his friend and college classmate, Mr. Charles Dudley Warner, he hastened to offer his services to Governor Buckingham as the first volunteer from Connecticut in defense of the flag and the Union. I was wont, as were many others in those stirring times, to visit the newspaper offices in quest of news. On one of the early days of June, when in the office of the *Press*, and in a conversation with Mr. Warner, it occurred to me that the birthday anniversary of the flag was near. I suggested to Mr. Warner the propriety of celebrating the day by public demonstration. He at once fell in with the idea. I said the flag and the Constitution were both on trial, and it was the duty of every loyal man to sustain them. Mr. Warner said he would write an article on the subject, and he did so in an editorial in the *Press* of the 8th of June, in which he advocated the establishment of the 14th day of June and the 17th day of September as national holidays, the one to be known as "Flag Day," the other as "Constitution Day."

We talked of the manner in which these days should be celebrated. We said we would leave the snap of the firecracker, the crack of the musket, the roar of cannon, and all the noise and racket which characterizes the Fourth of July to "Independence Day." Our "Flag Day" should be quiet. It would come at a season of the year when nature is rich in foliage and bloom, and when time is most enjoyable for out-of-door pleasures, and so parties, picnics, excursions should form part of the pleasures of the day. It should be a day of banners and decorations, but above and more beautiful than all should wave the Stars and Stripes of the Union. We said we would decorate our persons, our houses, and everything with flowers; that the world should bloom with beauty and be filled with fragrance. We said we would crown youth and old age with garlands, and every face should be radiant with joy. We said that night should be aglow with the candle, the rocket, and the gleam of the tinted lantern, and then when the festive day was over, we would go to our rest amidst sweet slumbers and dreams of Arcadian days. Such was our early idea of "Flag Day." Mr. Warner's suggestion for the observance of the day was well taken by the citizens of Hartford. There was a very general display of flags and decorations,—the "red, white, and blue" was displayed everywhere: from shops and houses; the dry goods stores vied with each other in their efforts at decoration. Other cities and towns had their celebrations also.

I do not know what was done here in Old Lebanon, but I know that your neighbors in Columbia did celebrate the day. The custom was kept up in more or less degree for some time, but with the exception of the display of flags there has been but little attempt to celebrate otherwise. A year passed away, and by June, 1862, the flag which had been deserted, pulled down, and disgraced in several of the States was again raised in them, and the authority of the Union partially restored. Early in this month I wrote to Hon. Dwight Loomis, then a member of Congress from this State, asking him to introduce in Congress a resolution for the observance of "Flag Day" as a national holiday, to embrace "Constitution Day" also. He readily complied with my request. I very much regret that I am left to tell this story of Congressional action. I hoped that Judge Loomis would have remained to tell it himself, but on account of the lateness of the hour he has been obliged to leave. Mr. Loomis introduced the following joint resolution on the 12th of June, and it was taken up in the order of business on the 13th:

"WHEREAS, The Continental Congress, on the 14th day of June, 1777, adopted the present flag of the United States, and the convention for the formation of a Constitution for the United States, on the 17th day of September, 1787, adopted our present Constitution; and whereas, that Constitution and flag, dear to us as the organic law and symbol of the Union which our fathers established, and which we have so long loved, have become more endeared to us by the toils and sacrifices which we are at this day called upon to undergo, and which we cheerfully accept, to preserve our national existence and the union of States; and whereas we desire, by an annual commemoration, to express our affection for our Constitution and flag, and to teach that affection to after generations; therefore,

"*Resolved by the Senate and House of Representatives of the United States of America, in Congress assembled,* That we recommend to the people of the United States to observe the 14th day of June and the 17th day of September in each year as national holidays — the first to be known as Flag Day, and the latter as Constitution Day."

Speaking on this resolution, Mr. Loomis said he offered it in good faith, believing that its adoption would do good; that it was worthy of the sanction of the House, and would meet with hearty response from loyal hearts throughout the land. If adopted, we should have three patriotic days commemorative of three important events in our national history — Independence Day, Flag Day, and Constitution Day — the first to commemorate the anniversary of our national independence; the second to commemorate the birthday of the national flag, for it was on the 14th day of June that the Continental Congress passed the resolution creating the flag, which resolution was:

"*Resolved*, That the flag of the United States be thirteen stripes, alternately red and white, and that the Union be thirteen stars, white on a blue field, representing a new constellation."

The third holiday — the 17th of September — would commemorate the adoption of the Constitution. These holidays, Mr. Loomis said, would be none too many; that, indeed, we had too few. The days named were worthy of commemoration. The glorious memories of the past, and the contest for the preservation of the

Union and Constitution united in rendering the days doubly dear through all future time to the American people. Mr. Loomis spoke with great eloquence and earnestness, and as no one desired to speak on the subject, he called the previous question. One would have supposed that the resolution, offered in good faith and in such patriotic spirit, in a time when both flag and constitution were undergoing the severest trial, would have been received without cavil or ridicule; that it would have been welcomed as a stimulant to the cause of the Union. How was it received? Mr. Thomas of Massachusetts suggested that the celebration of the 17th of September be funeral services of the Constitution; Mr. Hutchins of Ohio suggested that it be referred to the Committee on Judiciary. Mr. Thomas suggested it be referred to the special committee on the bankrupt law. Mr. Mallory of Kentucky thought it ought to go to the special committee on emancipation. Mr. E. B. Washburne of Illinois was opposed to any more holidays, and moved to lay the resolution on the table. The question was taken, and there was, on a division: Ayes 67, noes 33. So the resolution was laid on the table. Such was the temper of the House of Representatives, and such was the fate of "Flag Day" in that Congress. They thought it was a sentimental thing unworthy of the notice and favor of practical men. Then they wanted no more holidays. There was one holiday — the Fourth of July — that was enough for the people. Only Congress needs holidays. We know that the average Congressman always takes a holiday for a fortnight at Christmas, and then as much more just before election to go home for the purpose of "mending his fences" — that is a practical use of time! There is no waste or sentiment in that! Well, those men in Congress who were so opposed to sentiment and holidays are all gone; they have all passed away. They lived, however, to see a little more of both. They lived to hear the chant and song of the Union soldier in camp or on his march to the battlefield. They heard his shout of "We'll Rally 'round the Flag, Boys," and "Down with the Traitor and up with the Stars." They lived to see him on his homeward march, bearing aloft the dear old flags, torn, bullet-riddled, and begrimed and scorched with the smoke and fire of many battles — the battle flags.

> "Nothing but flags, but simple flags,
> Tattered and torn and hanging in rags;
> Baptized in blood, our purest, best,
> Tattered and torn, they're now at rest."

They lived to see the Union restored, and its banner waving in victory, and in the sunlight of peace, in the old places from which it had been driven. They lived to see the centennial of its natal day in 1877 celebrated throughout the land, and they saw that all this was something more than sentiment. There was a meaning in it. It was sincerity, love, devotion, the expression of true patriotism. They lived to see more holidays established — to see the birthday of Washington commemorated, on which we recount the deeds, the virtues, and wisdom of the father of his country; and Memorial Day and Thanksgiving Day — our old New England festival nationalized. And they lived to see Labor claiming its day for recognition and rest. And Judge Loomis has lived to see all this, and more. He has lived to see the old flag flying, by official order, every day from every public building, and from nearly every schoolhouse in the land — an object lesson in childhood; an educational force in the school of patriotism. And he is here to-day, to join in celebrating its birthday with the sons of those who fought to sustain it at its birth, and who followed it in victory through the Revolution. In connection with the celebration of the centennial of the flag in 1877, let me state that a distinguished editor in the Southwest, Hon. Henry Watterson of Louisville, Kentucky, had on Memorial Day, that year, in an address at Nashville, paid a beautiful tribute to "the starry flag of the Republic." I wrote to him thanking him for the spirit of his address, and suggested the observance of Flag Day that year, and the making of the day a national holiday. He was absent from home when my letter arrived, and did not return until after the day had passed. On his return he wrote me that he thought the suggestion an admirable one.

The National Society of the Sons of the American Revolution have authorized the commemoration of " Flag Day" by the State societies, and here to old Lebanon the Connecticut Society has come to celebrate the day. And what more fitting place could they have chosen? Lebanon! the home of patriots; the home of the Trumbulls, the Williams, the Clarks, and others. Lebanon! where so many plans were made and measures taken to carry on the revolution. Lebanon! soil trodden by Washington, Knox, and Trumbull; by Lafayette, Rochambeau, Tiernay, De Lauzun, and Chastellux, brave allies of the American cause.

Here in the old War Office of Brother Jonathan they held councils which led to victory. Here on the spot where we are gathered, and on the broad field before us, the golden lilies of France bloomed in beauty on their white banners beside the stars and stripes of America. Surely no spot is more sacred to Liberty than this! There was no place in the whole land where the principles of the Revolution were better understood and maintained than here.

This whole section was filled with the spirit of liberty. No two counties in the thirteen colonies did more for the patriot cause than the counties of New London and Windham. Certainly none furnished proportionately more soldiers for the army. I have wondered, Mr. President, why this was so, but when I remember the fact that the early settlers here were those, and the descendants of those, who in the old Bay opposed the oppressive measures of Charles I, and James II, I no longer wonder. Here, too, came men from the

Old Colony, — the Brewsters, the Bradfords, the Robinsons, the Hinckleys, and the Bartletts. The seed of the *Mayflower* was widely scattered here, and at the outbreak of the Revolution the compact signed in its cabin had not been forgotten. Then other influences were instrumental in the formation of the patriotic spirit. The clergymen of this section were all imbued with it. Here in Lebanon was Rev. Solomon Williams, father of the signer of the Declaration, and Thomas Brockway; in Norwich was Joseph Strong and Benjamin Lord; in Griswold, Levi Hart; in Woodstock, Abial Leonard; in Stonington, Nathaniel Ells; and down in Lyme, Rev. Stephen Johnson, the "incomparable" Stephen Johnson, whose pen was so prolific and powerful in the patriotic cause.

Then there were the two newspapers,— The New London *Gazette*, published by the fearless Timothy Greene, who dared to face the stamp act by issuing his paper unstamped; and the Norwich *Packet*, under John Trumbull, who sent away his Tory partners to New York to find more congenial society. All these contributed towards moulding public opinion; so, under these influences, there was not room for Tories to flourish, and there was not very much trouble with them. In fact there were only two or three of any note. Rev. Sam Peters, up in Hebron, was the most bitter and spiteful of them; but the Sons of Liberty took care of him. Rev. Mather Byles, in New London, didn't make much trouble, nor did Colonel Godfrey Malborne, up in Brooklyn.

But I have digressed. Well, our dream of "Flag Day" has not been realized in all its features. We were not as correct in our prophecy as was John Adams of Independence Day! Time has changed our programme. Another day has come into our calendar. If we have failed to weave garlands for youth and old age on "Flag Day," on "Memorial Day" we decorate with flowers and wreaths the graves of the fallen brave —

fallen in defense of the flag. This is now the duty of the living, and will be after the last veteran of the civil war shall have gone to his rest.

We need all these national holidays — never so much as now. We are absorbing into our social and political system hordes from other lands whom we must instruct and educate in the principles and institutions of our country, if we wish to preserve them; and we must continually refresh our studies of them ourselves. If "eternal vigilance is the price of liberty," that vigilance must be stimulated by the memories of the past. For the love of our country, we must forsake the pursuit of pleasure and wealth, and devote ourselves to duties of patriotism. As citizens, we can make no better use of time.

And the flag! In what better way can we tell its story. We hardly know its early history; the theories in regard to it are hardly tenable. Only the poet has divined its origin:

> "When Freedom from her mountain height,
>   Unfurled her standard to the air,
> She tore the azure robe of night
>   And set the stars of glory there.
> She mingled with its gorgeous dyes
>   The milky baldric of the skies;
> And striped its pure celestial white,
>   With streakings of the morning light.
> Then from his mansion in the sun
>   She called her eagle-bearer down,
> And gave into his mighty hand
>   The symbol of her chosen land."

We may well believe its bright stars were a gift from the constellations; its stripes from the rays of the morning, sent to herald and lighten the day of liberty to the world.

The old flag! It is something more than a harmonious arrangement of beautiful colors. It means something. It represents something. It is indeed the signal of liberty. Its bright stripes bear the record of a protest against tyranny and oppression. It enfolds the history of constitutional liberty and free government. Henceforth its birthday will be remembered as the years come around. The dear old flag! Glorious as has been its past, its future shall be more glorious still. Brighter and brighter shall its stars shine, and more and more brilliant shall its stripes glow. Over broader lands and wider seas and on greater heights shall its glory spread and its victories be won.

The President: This occasion would not be complete if we should fail to hear the voice of a well-known and well-beloved son of Lebanon, the brother of the second war-governor whom this honored town has furnished to our State and country. I have the pleasure and honor to inform the audience that the Rev. Dr. Samuel G. Buckingham has kindly consented to address us.

DR. BUCKINGHAM'S ADDRESS.

Mr. President and People of Connecticut:

I am not, I suppose, one of the Sons of the Revolution, but I claim to be a true and loyal son of Connecticut. Though I have spent all my professional life in Massachusetts, and cherish the profoundest respect for her institutions and people, still I was born and trained here. Our ancestor was one of the original settlers of the New Haven Colony, and one of his sons bore a leading part in the organization of your churches and in the founding and rectorship of Yale College. And familiar as I am with your achievements, is it strange that I honor and love my native State? Especially since you selected my brother to be your Governor, when the war for the Union was coming on, and so nobly sustained him and the Union until all opposition to it was put down, and slavery, the cause of all our dissensions, was forever removed, do you wonder that my heart turns admiringly and gratefully to you, and always will under whatever skies I may chance to find myself? Since the State put $2,000,000 at his disposal at the outset of the war for the purposes of the war, and at his suggestion loaned the credit of the State to the General Government to sustain its credit, and furnished soldiers at his call till every quota called for was supplied without ever submitting to a draft, and when you withheld not your noblest sons from the sacrifices of war, and so many of them went forth never to return,—can one brought up among them, with their principles in his heart, if not their blood in his veins, fail to admire them and the State that trained them to be such patriots?

God's best gift to Lebanon was its first settlers. Captain Joseph Trumbull, the first of the name here, and the founder of the Lebanon branch of the family, settled here in 1704, just after the town was organized. He was a farmer and a merchant, and subsequently engaged, with his sons, in foreign commerce, building vessels of their own on the Thames and the Connecticut, and exchanging their exports for imports from the West Indies, England, and Holland. He had eight children, four sons and four daughters, of whom his oldest son, Joseph, his partner in business and supercargo of one of their ships, was lost at sea, and David, the youngest, was drowned in the mill-pond at home on his college vacation. Jonathan, the "War Governor," had just graduated from college and finished his preparation for the ministry, and was to have been settled in Colchester, when his brother was lost at sea, and he felt constrained to abandon the ministry and go to the assistance of his father. Here he acquired that business knowledge and ability which proved so valuable when he came to administer the affairs of the State and succor Washington and his army in their extremity. No wonder General Washington looked to him with hope when he could find help nowhere else, saying, "Let us see what Brother Jonathan can do for us": and little wonder that he found it when the State responded with such contributions and sacrifices to the appeals of their heroic Governor.

The Governor's own family was as follows:

JOSEPH, born March, 1737, was Commissary-General of Washington's army.

JONATHAN, JR., born March 26, 1740, was Paymaster in Washington's army, and afterwards Governor of the State.

FAITH, born Jan. 25, 1743, married Gen. Jedediah Huntington, of the Revolutionary army.

MARY, born July 16, 1745, married William Williams, "signer of the Declaration of Independence."

DAVID, born Feb. 5, 1751, was Assistant Commissary, etc., and father of Governor Joseph.

JOHN, born June 6, 1756, was Aid-de-Camp to Washton, and the renowned painter.

To say that this whole family filled so many high positions with distinguished ability and fidelity; that the father filled every civil and judicial office of the State, from one of the deputies of the town to the General Court, to the speakership of the House of Representatives, and from Judge of Probate to the office of the Chief Justice of the Superior and Supreme Courts, before he became Governor; that the sons all filled their military offices with honor, and especially in departments which required the highest financial integrity and ability, and when the youngest showed such peculiar aptitude for the military profession, and yet turned away from it to become the historical painter of his country, and make the panels of the Capitol at Washington the memorial of his genius; and that the daughters each adorned her sphere with equal grace and patriotism; and, to say no more, is honor enough for one household.

Add to this the WILLIAMS family, that married into the Trumbull family. Rev. Solomon Williams, D.D., who was for fifty-four years the pastor here, belonged to the family of those who suffered the barbarities of captivity that attended the burning of Deerfield by the Indians in 1704. One of his sons, Eliphalet, was pastor of the church in East Hartford some fifty years, and another, Ezekiel, was for thirty years high sheriff of Hartford county, and he the father of one of the Chief Justices of Connecticut. Dr. Williams might well have been the father of one of the signers of the Declaration of Independence, judging from the jubilant sermon he preached on the surrender of Quebec in 1759, when a general thanksgiving was observed, and he so well appreciated the importance of it, regarding "the conquest of Quebec, the capital of Canada, as of more importance than has ever been made by the English since England was a nation." His son William, — usually styled Colonel William Williams — the one who immortalized himself by signing that Declaration of Independence, graduated at Harvard College and studied for the ministry with his father, but joined the English and Continental forces in the old French war, on the staff of his cousin, Colonel Ephraim Williams, who fell in that campaign. Of ardent temperament, beautiful in person, eloquent of speech, and capable of inspiring others with his own convictions and patriotism, he went over the State arousing the people to their danger and their duty, while his brother-in-law, David Trumbull, was buying up all the pork in the State, and collecting gunpowder and clothing from every quarter, to enable our poor army to keep the field. The man who would risk his life to secure our independence, and impoverished himself to maintain the cause, might well be regarded as the apostle of Liberty, and the most efficient supporter of the patriotic Governor. When the outlook was darkest, and one of the Council of Safety expressed the hope that we might yet be successful, he replied: "If we fail, I know what my fate will be. I have done much to prosecute the war, and one thing which the British will never pardon, I have signed the Declaration of Independence. *I shall be hung!*" "Well," said another member of the Council, "if we fail, I don't know that I could be hung. For my name is not attached to that Declaration, nor have I written anything against the British government." "Then," said Williams, "*you ought to be hung for not doing your duty.*" As has been said of him: "With tongue, pen, and estate he gave himself to the cause of the colonies. During the gloomy winter of 1777 he sent beef, cattle, and gold to Valley Forge, saying, 'If independence shall be established, I shall get my pay; if not, the loss will be of no account to me.'"

Another of those families was the MASON family, not only distinguished by their natural characteristics and practical ability, but by their high descent. They were the descendants of Major John Mason, of Pequot fame, and the first proprietor of land within the limits of the town. The Colony gave him for his services five hundred acres of land, and much more was purchased of the Indians, until he was the chief proprietor of the whole township. Fifty years ago, three of his descendants, two sons and a daughter, with large families, were influential people in the town, and not only noted for their noble personal appearance, but as well for their business ability and public spirit. Another of them was Jeremiah Mason, the famous Massachusetts lawyer, and contemporary of Mr. Webster, who paid such a beautiful tribute before the Boston bar to his abilities and worth. But the most remarkable characteristic of this family was — as has been shown in Chancellor Walworth's "Genealogy of the Hyde Family" (Vol. II, page 926) — that they were descended from William the Conqueror, from the Plantagenets of England, Matilda of Scotland, Louis the Fair of France, and from Charlemagne, the great Emperor of the West, and with blue blood enough in their veins to stock a kingdom.

Such were some of the people who had the early guidance of affairs and the shaping of public sentiment in this New England town. And such were some of the moulding influences which made the State what it was and shaped our general government; and wherever they have been carried by emigration, must have been a blessing, as they have been here.* The springs where mountain streams take their rise, and flow down through fertile plains, and alongside of wealthy cities, to enrich the commerce of the world, and bless its countless inhabitants, are interesting spots to visit, and suggestive of what smaller towns may have done for the world and are likely to do in the future.

The *list of Governors* which this town has furnished to the State is certainly remarkable, both in number and character, especially considering its population and business. Entirely an agricultural town, with never more than three (3,000) thousand inhabitants, it has filled the chair of State with such men as these, and for such terms of office:

Jonathan Trumbull, Sr.,	1769 to 1784.
Jonathan Trumbull, Jr.,	1798 to 1809.
Clark Bissell,	1847 to 1849.
Joseph Trumbull,	1849 to 1850.
William A. Buckingham,	1858 to 1866.

Here are five Governors from the same town, holding the office by annual election for one-third of a century, and filling the office with becoming dignity and distinguished usefulness. We do not wonder at the pleasant boast of the people of the town:—" *We supply Norwich with butter and cheese, and the State with Governors, especially when they want good ones.*"

---

* When I was a boy, emigration from this town was going on to " 'hio,"— Ohio — " Genisee county," in and about Rochester, N. Y., and " up county," which meant Vermont. Dartmouth College, under Pres. Wheelock, then " Moore's Charity School " for the education of Indian youth, had been taken up almost bodily and transported from Columbia, then a part of this town, to Hanover, N. H., just across the river. And so many of the settlers went with it from this vicinity that twenty or more of the neighboring towns in Vermont bear the names of Connecticut towns from which the settlers came. Indeed, the State had so much of this settlement in it that it was named " New Connecticut," and the name was only changed because there were other settlements of similar origin taking the same name — like the " New Connecticut " in the Susquehanna Valley, and the " New Connecticut " of Northern Ohio, both of which distinctly show the characteristics of their origin.

The TRUMBULL TOMB, where so many of the family and their kindred sleep, is an object of peculiar interest. As has been said: " Within this family mausoleum rest the sacred ashes of more of the illustrious dead than in any other in the State, or perhaps the country. Here rest the remains of that eminently great and good Jonathan Trumbull, Sr., the bosom friend and most trusted counsellor of Washington; of his good wife, Faith Robinson; of his eldest son, Joseph, the first Commissary-General of the army under Washington; of his second son, Jonathan, Jr., Paymaster-General of the same army, private secretary, and first Aid-de-Camp to General Washington, and afterward Speaker of the United States House of Representatives, member of the United States Senate, and Governor of this State; and by his side his good wife, Eunice Backus; of his third son, David, Commissary of this Colony in the Revolution, and Assistant-Commissary-General under his brother in the army of Washington, and by his side his good wife, Sarah Backus; of his second daughter, Mary, and by her side her illustrious husband, William Williams, one of the signers of the immortal Declaration of Independence, — and many others who have from these descended. What a tomb is here! What a shrine for patriotic devotion!"
—[Rev. Mr. Hine's " Early Lebanon."]

As I have stood before that tomb with my brother, I can think of nothing so likely to have inspired him with his patriotism as this. Sure I am, that next to his duty to God, no stronger motive influenced him than the desire to be to his State and country somewhat such as Trumbull was in the War of the Revolution. And the heroic statue to his memory, which you have set up in your State Capitol, like the one erected to the honor of his predecessor in the National Capitol, will carry down their names together to posterity, the one as " *the War Governor of the Revolution,*" and the other as " *the War Governor of the Rebellion.*"

It is the memory of such spotless and noble characters; the places where they were born, and lie sleeping; the associations of their early lives, and the scenes of their active usefulness, which serve to influence and ennoble us. And it is to revive and deepen such impressions and transmit them to others that we gather in this old historic town, and set apart, with appropriate services, Governor Trumbull's War Office to such uses. It is only a plain wooden building, built by the Governor for a store, but where most of the twelve hundred sessions of the Council of Safety were held during the war. Here is where Washington and so many of the leading men of the times came to consult him, and where some of the important expeditions of the war were planned. It is generally understood that the meeting here of so many of the commanders of the French land forces and the officers of their navy with our own statesmen and commanders had reference to the combined expedition against Yorktown, which terminated the war, though the final determination might have been reached at "the Webb Tavern" in Wethersfield — a humble building, but ennobled by the great men who gathered there, the noble plans projected there, the great achievements carried out to their sublime results from such a place. It is the glory which sunshine gives to a humble flower; the glory of modest worth and faithful usefulness; the glory somewhat which Heaven sheds over a sainted soul : —

> "Sacred the robe, the faded glove,
> Once worn by one we used to love;
> Dead warriors in their armor live,
> And in their relics saints survive."

As we have thus re-read this chapter of your history, we have been more than ever impressed with the influence of individual characters and families and noble deeds upon a town, a State, the country. It is men and women that make history, and it is history, in turn, that makes them of coming generations; it is parents who transmit their own characteristics; it is the family that moulds the children; it is such characters and such families which are the wealth of the nation; it is their principles and achievements which are the cherished treasures of our State and of the country. And so we reckon them among God's best gifts to any community. But for these how changed would our condition be, and how different our history? If our old Puritan Governor had been no more patriotic than the rest of them; if his son-in-law had not affixed his signature to that immortal declaration; if his sons, in the commissary department of the army, had not been so efficient and incorruptible in the management of its affairs; if France had not sent Lafayette and her army and her navy to our assistance; if the last expedition of the war had not been planned in that old War Office — how changed would have been the result! And we are grateful to God — supremely grateful — for such a result. His Providence settled the town with such families, and trained such characters. The same good Providence gave us the sympathy and aid of the French nation. And the God of battles gave us the final victory. We bow with reverent and grateful hearts before this God of our fathers; and He shall be our God, as well as theirs, forever and ever.

At the conclusion of Dr. Buckingham's address, the benediction was pronounced by the Rev. S. Dryden Phelps, chaplain of the New Haven branch of the Society.

The audience then gradually dispersed in various directions, the band playing *Auld Lang Syne* as its closing piece.

APPENDIX.

The proclamation to which Dr. Bacon refers in his address is here given in full: —

"By the Honorable JONATHAN TRUMBULL, Esq Governor and Commander-in-chief of the English Colony of Connecticut in New England.

"A PROCLAMATION

"The Race of Mankind was made in a State of Innocence and Freedom subjected only to the Laws of God the Creator, and through his rich Goodness, designed for virtuous liberty and Happiness, here and forever; and when moral Evil was introduced into the World, and Man had corrupted his Ways before God, Vice and Iniquity came in like a Flood and Mankind became exposed, and a prey to the Violence, Injustice and Oppression of one another. God in great Mercy inclined his People to form themselves into Society, and to set up and establish civil Government for the Protection and security of their Lives and Properties from the Invasion of wicked men. But through Pride and ambition, the Kings and Princes of the World appointed by the People the Guardians of their Lives and Liberties, early and almost universally degenerated into Tyrants, and by Fraud or Force betrayed and wrested out of their hands the very Rights and Properties they were appointed to protect and defend. But a small part of the Human Race maintained and enjoyed any tolerable Degree of Freedom. Among those happy few, the nation of Great Britain was distinguished by a Constitution of Government wisely framed and modelled to support the Dignity and Power of the Prince, for the protection of the Rights of the People, and under which that Country in long succession enjoyed great Tranquillity and Peace, though not unattended with repeated and powerful efforts, by many of its haughty Kings, to destroy the Constitutional Rights of the People, and establish arbitrary Power and Dominion. In one of those convulsive struggles our Forefathers, having suffered in that their native Country great and variety of Injustice and Oppression, left their dear Connections and Enjoyments, and fled to this then inhospitable land to secure a lasting retreat from civil and religious Tyranny.

"The God of Heaven favored and prospered this Undertaking — made room for their settlement — increased and multiplied them to a very numerous People and inclined succeeding Kings to indulge them and their children for many years the unmolested Enjoyment of the Freedom and Liberty they fled to inherit. But an unnatural King has risen up — violated his sacred Obligations and by the Advice of Evil Counsellors attempted to wrest from us, their children the Sacred Rights we justly claim and which have been ratified and established by solemn Compact with, and recognized by his Predecessors and Fathers, Kings of *Great Britain* — laid upon us Burdens too heavy and grievous to be borne and issued many cruel and oppressive Edicts, depriving us of our natural, lawful and most important Rights, and subjecting us to the absolute Power and Controul of himself and the *British* Legislature; against which we have sought Relief, by humble, earnest and dutiful Complaints and Petitions: But, instead of obtaining Redress our Petitions have been treated with Scorn and Contempt, and fresh Injuries heaped upon us while hostile armies and ships are sent to lay waste our Country. In this distressing Dilemma, having no Alternative but absolute Slavery or successful Resistance, this, and the United American Colonies have been constrained by the overruling laws of Self Preservation to take up

Arms for the Defence of all that is sacred and dear to Freemen, and make this solemn Appeal to Heaven for the Justice of their Cause, and resist Force by Force.

"God Almighty has been pleased of his infinite Mercy to succeed our Attempts, and give us many Instances of signal Success and Deliverance. But the wrath of the King is still increasing, and not content with before employing all the Force which can be sent from his own Kingdom to execute his cruel Purposes, has procured, and is sending all the Mercenaries he can obtain from foreign countries to assist in extirpating the Rights of *America*, and with theirs almost all the liberty remaining among Mankind.

"In this most critical and alarming situation, this and all the Colonies are called upon and earnestly pressed by the Honorable Congress of the *American* Colonies united for mutual defence, to raise a large additional number of their militia and able men to be furnished and equipped with all possible Expedition for defence against the soon expected attack and invasion of those who are our Enemies without a Cause. In cheerful compliance with which request and urged by Motives the most cogent and important that can affect the human Mind, the General Assembly of this Colony have freely and unanimously agreed and resolved, that upwards of Seven Thousand able and effective Men be immediately raised, furnished and equipped for the great and interesting Purposes aforesaid. And not desirous that any should go to a warfare at their own charges (though equally interested with others) for defence of the great and all-important Cause in which we are engaged, have granted large and liberal Pay and Encouragements to all who shall voluntarily undertake for the Defence of themselves and their country as by their acts may appear, I do *therefore* by and with the advice of the Counsel, and at the desire of the Representatives in General Court assembled, issue this PROCLAMATION, and make the solemn Appeal to the Virtue and public Spirit of the good People of this Colony. Affairs are hastening fast to a Crisis, and the approaching Campaign will in all Probability determine forever the fate of AMERICA. If this should be successful on our side, there is little to fear on account of any other. Be exhorted to rise therefore to superior exertions on this great Occasion, and let all that are able and necessary show themselves ready in Behalf of their injured and oppressed Country, and come forth to the help of the Lord against the Mighty, and convince the unrelenting Tyrant of *Britain* that they are resolved to be *Free*. Let them step forth to defend their Wives, their little Ones, their Liberty, and everything they hold sacred and dear, to defend the Cause of their Country, their Religion, and their God. Let every one to the utmost of their Power lend a helping Hand, to promote and forward a design on which the salvation of *America* now evidently depends. Nor need any be dismayed: the Cause is certainly a just and a glorious one: God is able to save us in such way and manner as he pleases and to humble our proud Oppressors. The Cause is that of Truth and Justice; he has already shown his Power in our Behalf, and for the Destruction of many of our Enemies. *Our Fathers trusted in him and were delivered.* Let us all repent and thoroughly amend our Ways and turn to him, put all our Trust and Confidence in him — in his Name go forth, and in his Name set up our Banners, and he will save us with temporal and eternal salvation. And while our Armies are abroad jeoparding their lives in the high Places of the Field, let all who remain at Home, cry mightily to God for the Protection of his Providence to shield and defend their lives from Death, and to crown them with victory and success. And in the Name of the said General Assembly I do hereby earnestly recommend it to all, both Ministers and People frequently to meet together for social prayer to Almighty God for the outpouring of his blessed Spirit upon this guilty land — That he would awaken his People to Righteousness and Repentance, bless our Councils, prosper our Arms and succeed the Measures using for our necessary self defence disappoint the evil and cruel Devices of our Enemies preserve our precious Rights and Liberties, lengthen out our Tranquility, and make us a People of his Praise, and the blessed of the Lord, as long as the Sun and Moon shall endure.

"And all the Ministers of the Gospel in this Colony, are directed and desired, to publish this Proclamation in their several churches and congregations, and to enforce the Exhortations thereof, by their own pious Example and public instructions.

"*Given under my Hand at the Council Chamber in Hartford, the 18th day of June Anno Domini 1776.*

"JONATHAN TRUMBULL."

Regarding this proclamation, Dr. Charles J. Hoadly, in an unpublished letter, writes as follows:

"In May, 1776, the convention of Virginia passed certain resolutions instructing their delegates in Congress to propose to that respectable body to declare the United American Colonies Free and Independent States, and ordered copies to be communicated to each of the other Colonies. There was a special session of the Connecticut General Assembly held June 14–21, 1776. With other papers, the Virginia resolves were laid before it. On the forenoon of the 15th, a joint committee was raised to consider the expediency of instructing our delegates in Congress to declare the United Colonies independent States. This committee reported a preamble and resolves very closely echoing those of Virginia, which passed *unanimously*. The proclamation by Gov. Trumbull was dated the 18th. It is probable that it had passed both Houses like a bill—at least, that would have been the usual course then."

This proclamation is also mentioned in the diary of Major French in Vol. I of the *Collections of the Connecticut Historical Society*.

Regarding the Trumbull papers in possession of the Massachusetts Historical Society, the following items are of interest:

At its May Session of 1771, the General Assembly of Connecticut passed the following resolution:

"That his Honor the Governor be desired to collect all the publick letters and papers which may hereafter in any way affect the interest of this Colony, and have the same bound together that they may be preserved." (*Colonial Records of Connecticut, Vol. XIII, page 424.*)

In a foot note referring to this resolution, Dr. Charles J. Hoadly, the editor, says:

"Of the papers collected by Governor Trumbull under this resolution, his son David in 1794 presented to the Massachusetts Historical Society a great number, which are now in the possession of that society, known as the *Trumbull Papers*, and bound in thirty volumes. Another volume, containing papers of an earlier date than 1751, was destroyed by a fire in 1825. Some of these papers have been published in various volumes of the society's *Collections*; the recently printed Vol. IX of the fourth series consists entirely of the so-called *Trumbull Papers*.

"Pursuant to a resolve of the May session, 1845, a claim was made to these papers as belonging to the archives of Connecticut. Some of the correspondence on the subject may be seen in Vol. II of the *Proceedings of the Massachusetts Historical Society*. The demand was not acknowledged by the society, on the ground that, in their opinion, the papers were the private property of Gov. Trumbull, and that his heirs had the right to dispose of them at their pleasure.

"Of the volume lately printed, above referred to, pages 213-490 contain letters of William Samuel Johnson to the Governors of Connecticut during his agency in England, 1766-71. The book from which these were taken is described in the prefatory editorial note to the volume of *Collections*, page x, as being already bound when it came into the society's possession. In our archives, *Finance and Currency,* v. doc. 82 a, is Gov. Trumbull's account of contingent expenses rendered in 1774, one item in which is Mr. Green's charge of 5s. 6d. 'for binding Dr. Johnson's Letters.'"

This note of Dr. Hoadly was printed in 1885. Since then, in 1888, another volume of the "*Trumbull Papers*" has been published by the *Massachusetts Historical Society* in Vol. X, fifth series, containing, mainly, "*Trumbull and Washington Letters.*"

A well-authenticated story of the wife of David Trumbull forms one of the many illustrations of the patriotic spirit of the women of the Revolution, and seems worthy of a place in this connection.

In the winter of 1780-81, at a time when Lauzun's French Legion was on the march for its quarters in Lebanon, the question of providing accommodations for the officers became a serious one. Accustomed to every luxury at home, they were expected to need the most luxurious quarters which Lebanon could afford. As the time for their arrival drew near, the question was still agitating the plain people of Lebanon. But one house in the town boasted a carpet, used as an ornament, with an ample border of bare floor for the family to tread upon to save the wear of the carpet, which rare decoration was in a large room in the house of the Governor's son, David, who had then been married scarcely three years to Sarah Backus of Norwich, who was just a year his junior.

In the emergency just mentioned, the Governor asked his son, David, if he would give up his house to the French officers,— Rochambeau, the Baron de Stael, the Duke de Lauzun, and others, Lafayette being also expected as an occasional visitor. To this, the son very properly replied that he must consult Mrs. Trumbull, which he proceeded at once to do. To the question, "Will you allow me to take you to your mother's house at Norwich, and give up our house to the French officers?" Mrs. Trumbull promptly replied, "Certainly." She was informed that the troops were already on the march, and was asked when she would be ready for her journey. "In just one hour," was the prompt reply; and at the appointed time, with her infant daughter, fifteen months old, leaving everything in the way of comforts in her house, this patriotic lady set out for her drive of twelve miles on a cold December day. On the second day of the following January, her second daughter, Abigail, was born at Norwich.

During the following April, while Lafayette was at Lebanon, Mrs. Trumbull paid a visit to her home. Lafayette requested that he might see the "patriotic lady" and her "patriotic baby." He met them at the door of their own house, and taking the baby in his arms kissed it tenderly and handed it about to the other officers. A portion of a brocade dress which Mrs. Trumbull wore on this occasion is still preserved as a family heirloom.

Although the story of the contribution of a cloak by her mother-in-law, Faith Trumbull, may be more thrilling on account of the dramatic situation at the time, the actual sacrifice of the daughter-in-law to the cause will certainly bear comparison.

The following editorial comments from the Hartford *Courant* of June 16, 1891, form a just and fitting tribute to the occasion, and to the town and people of Lebanon:

"LEBANON'S GREAT CELEBRATION.

"It was a great day for Lebanon, Monday, and a good one for Connecticut, too. Every day is good that tends to revive and quicken the local pride of our Connecticut towns, and surely that must have resulted from Monday's celebration in Lebanon. This old town has furnished governors for the State through thirty-six of our one hundred and fifteen years of statehood. There was old Brother Jonathan's headquarters, and in that central and thriving community, right on the highway to Boston, a vast amount of the work was done that brought the Revolutionary war to its successful issue.

"All this picture of the past was vividly recalled, Monday, both by the occasion and the admirable speeches, and all who were present had their patriotism profoundly stirred. Lebanon has become a 'back town.' It is on the same road as of old, but that is no longer the great highway to Boston. The town is still given to agriculture; and farming, they tell us, is played out, and the soil of Connecticut is being worked by those who are strangers to it.

"The town of Lebanon furnished its own answer, Monday, to these charges. The farming people were there, and they were a genuine American crowd — sober, interested, orderly, intelligent, the strength of the State. To say that the back towns are degenerating when such people make up the bulk of their population is to ignore facts. Brother Jonathan himself, great man as he was in many ways, would have found himself at home and at his ease could he have visited Lebanon, Monday, and, while the material changes might have seemed strange to him, the people would have been of the sort he knew and trusted."

INDEX.

Abell, Charles J., 21.
Abell, Mrs. Myron, 22.
Adams, John, 33.
Adams, Samuel, 33, 49.
Adams, 54.
Almy, Dr. Leonard B., 20.
Andrews, President E. B., 61.
Arnold, 50, 53.
Arnoux, Hon. William H., 61.
Avery, David, 36.
Avery, Deacon John D., 36.
Avery, John H., 22, 23.
Avery, Mrs. W. B., 23.
Backus, Eunice, 80.
Backus, Sarah, 80, 89.
Bacon, Rev. Dr. Leonard, 44.
Bacon, Rev. Dr. Leonard W., 24, 42, 43, 83.
Ball, George Washington, 61.
Barker, Mrs. Maria F., 22.
Barker, N. C., 21.
Barrett, Hon. Edwin S., 60.
Bayard, Hon. Thomas F., 57.
Beaumonts, The, 43.
Bissell, Clark, 79.
Boston, 5, 6, 7, 45, 46.
Bowen, Clarence W., 61.
Bradfords, The, 72.
Branford, 15.
Brewsters, The, 72.
Briggs, Mrs. Annie E., 22.
Briggs, Mrs. C. S., 23.
Brockway, Thomas, 72.
Brooklyn, 72.
Brown, Gov. Montford, 17.
Brown, Mrs. Frederick, 22.
Browning, Miss Cecil, 22.
Bryce, Dr., 44.
Buchanan, John W., 59.
Buckingham, Rev. Dr. Samuel G., 74, 82.
Buckingham, Gov. William A., 79.
Bulkeley, Gov. Morgan G., 37.
Bunker Hill, 36, 47.
Burgess, Mrs. R. P., 22, 23.
Butts, Charles R., 20.
Byles, Rev. Mather, 72.
Cabell, Hon. William D., 59.
Cadwalader, Richard M., 61.
Camp, Capt. Abiather, 17.
Carroll, Adams P., 20.
Chase, Hon. Champion S., 59.
Chastellux, Marquis de, 53.
Clark, Mrs. John, 22.
Cheney, Rt. Rev. Charles E., 61.
Clark, Mrs. Henry, 22.
Cleveland, ex-President Grover, 61.
Coit, Rev. Dr. Henry A., 61.
Collier, Thomas S., 24, 38.
Colonial Records, 8, 19, 88.
Connecticut, 43, 44, 45, 46, 49, 52, 57.
Conn. Historical Society, 14, 15, 19, 20, 24, 26, 87.
Conn. Society Sons of the Am. Revolution, 11, 19, 20, 21, 24, 25, 26, 29, 30, 33, 45.
Constitution Day, 66, 67, 68.
Cornwallis, 36.
Council of Safety, 8, 9, 14, 15, 16, 17, 18, 19, 49, 77.
Crandall, Hon. John C., 21.
Darling, Mrs. F. A., 61.
Dartmouth College, 79.
Delaplace, Capt., 15.
Declaration of Independence, 25, 32, 52.

Dewey, Noah, 13, 14.
Dolbeare, Miss S. M., 23.
Durham, 17.
Dutton, Miss Mary H., 12, 26.
Dwight, President Timothy, 61.
Dyer, Eliphalet, 7.
East Hartford, 76.
Edgerton, Hon. Albert, 60.
Elderkin, Jedidiah, 7.
Eliot, President Charles W., 61.
Ells, Nathaniel, 72.
Fairfield, 50.
Favor, Mrs., 27.
Favor, Prof., 27.
Fiske, John, 50.
Fitch, 48.
Flag Day, 20, 24, 64, 66, 67, 68, 71.
Fort Sumter, 65.
Fowler, Amos, 35.
Fowler, Col. Anson, 35, 36, 38.
Fowler, Frank P., 21.
Fowler, John, 36.
Franklin, Benjamin, 16, 33.
Franklin, Gen. William B., 61.
Franklin, Gov. William, 13, 16, 18.
Freeman's Journal, 13.
French, Major, 15, 87.
Gage, Gov., 46.
Gardiner, Major Asa Bird, 61.
Gates, W. F., 21, 22.
Gates, Mrs. W. F., 22.
Geer, Erastus, 22, 35, 37.
Geer, Mrs. Erastus, 22.
General Assembly, 7, 8, 14, 17, 19, 86, 87, 88.
Gibbs, Mrs. Edward, 23.
Gillett, Mrs. William W., 22.
Gilman, President Daniel C., 59.
Glassenbury, Town of, 13.
Glastenbury, 17.
Greene, Hon. Nathanael, 60.
Greene, Timothy, 72.
Griswold, Hon. Mathew, 7, 8.
Griswold (town), 72.
Groton Massacre, 36, 50, 51.
Guilliver, Rev. Dr. John P., 60.

Hale, Rev. Dr. Edward Everett, 58.
Halsey, Jeremiah, 20.
Hamilton, William G., 58.
Harrison, 54.
Hart, Levi, 72.
Hartford, 15, 26, 67.
Hartford Courant, 90.
Hawley, Gen. Joseph R., 24, 27, 65.
Haynes, 45.
Hebron, 72.
Henry, Patrick, 49.
Henry, Hon. William Wirt, 57.
Hewitt, E. W., 21.
Hewitt, Miss Hattie E., 22.
Hill, Hon. E. J., 57.
Hinckleys, The, 72.
Hinman, 8.
Hoadly, Dr. Charles J., 8, 52, 87, 88, 89.
Hooker, Thomas, 44, 45.
Hoxie, Miss Minnie, 22.
Hutchins, Hon., of Ohio, 69.
Hutchinson, Gov., 47.
Huntington, Benjamin, 7.
Huntington, Rt. Rev. F. D., 60.
Huntington, J. L. W., 20.
Huntington, Jabez, 7, 27, 52.
Huntington, Samuel, 7.
Hyde, Burrell W., 20.
Irish, Mrs. Phebe C., 22.
Isaacs, Ralph, 13, 16, 17, 18.
James Island, 65.
Jefferson, 33, 52.
Johnson, Stephen, 72.
Johnson, William Samuel, 6, 7, 88, 89.
Johnston, Alexander, 44.
Keep, Dr. Robert P., 20.
King, John S., 21.
Kingsley, John D., 36.
Kingsley, Ashael, 36.
Kneeland, Mrs. A. G., 22.
Knox, 9, 33.
Lafayette, 9, 82, 89, 90.
Lauzun, Duke de, 9, 10, 25, 50, 53, 54, 89.
Learned, Major B. P., 20.

Leavens, F. J., 20.
Lebanon, 5, 6, 7, 8, 9, 10, 11, 16, 20, 21, 24, 25, 30, 34, 35, 43, 50, 51, 54, 56, 61, 62, 63, 67, 80, 90, 91.
Ledyard, John, 13, 14.
Leonard, Abiel, 72.
Litchfield, 16.
Loan Exhibition, 24, 25.
Loomis, Hon. Dwight, 64, 67, 68, 69, 70.
Loomis, Mrs. L. P., 23.
Loomis, W. B., 21.
Love, Rev. William deLoss, 24, 30.
Long Island, Battle of, 17, 36.
Ludlow, 45.
Ludlow, R. Fulton, 61.
Lyman, Mrs. G. W., 22.
Lyman, Mrs. L. L., 23.
Lyme, 72.
Malborne, Col. Godfrey, 72.
Mallory, Hon. Mr., of Kentucky, 69.
Manley, Miss Hattie J., 22.
Mason, Col. John, 78.
Mason, Jeremiah, 78.
Massachusetts, 44, 45, 46.
Massachusetts Historical Society, 14, 88.
McCall, Mrs. Hobart, 23.
Middletown, 16.
Mills, George A., 22.
Mills, Mrs. George A., 22, 23.
Minerva, The, 18.
Mitchell, Donald G., 53.
Moffit, Mrs. Edward, 22.
Mohegan Case, 6, 7.
Moland, Ensign Joseph, 13, 14, 15.
Montgomery, James M., 61.
Moore's Charity School, 79.
Morgan, Capt. Griswold E., 37.
Morgan, George H., 37.
Morgan, Gov., of N. Y., 37.
Morgan, Nathaniel H., 8.
Morgan, William Avery, 37.
Morgan, William E., 37.
Morris, Jonathan F., 15, 31, 64.
Morton, Hon. Levi P., 57.

New Connecticut, 79.
New Haven, 13, 17, 18, 26, 50.
New Jersey, 13, 16.
New London, 36, 51, 72.
New London County, 71.
New Providence, 17.
Norwalk, 50.
Norwich, 8, 20, 25, 26, 54, 72, 90.
Nott, Dr., 26.
Noyes, Frank K., 21.
Noyes, Mrs. F. K., 22.
Nye, Mrs. George A., 22, 23.
Parks, The, 43.
Parsons, 9.
Perit, J., 16.
Peckham, C. H., 23.
Peters, Rev. Samuel, 72.
Pettis, Mrs. Nancy E., 23.
Phelps, Hon. Edward J., 61.
Phelps, Rev. S. Dryden, 82.
Pitcher, C. L., 21.
Pitkin, Governor, 6, 7.
Post, A. R., 21.
Prindle, Miss Helen O., 22.
Proctor, Hon. Redfield, 61.
Provision State, 9.
Pumpelly, J. C., 59.
Putnam, 33.
Randall, Mrs. L. H., 23.
Raymond, George C., 20.
Revere, Paul, 58.
Robinsons, The, 72.
Robinson, Faith, 80.
Robinson, Mrs. Charles, 22.
Robinson, Miss Louise, 23.
Robinson, Mrs. William, 23.
Rochambeau, 9, 10, 50, 53, 89.
Rotton, Ensign, 15.
Rousseau, Jean Jacques, 52.
Roustan, Theodore, French Minister, 57.
Russell, Hon. Charles A., 61, 62.
Skene, Major, 15.
Smith, L. P., 21, 22.
Spaulding, Mrs. L. A., 22.
Spencer, 9.

Staël, Baron de, 80.
Standish, Clark, 21.
Stark, Miss Masey E., 22
Starr, Frank Farnsworth, 11
Stebbins, Mrs. H. D., 23.
Stedman, Joe, 23.
Stiles, Mrs. Edward A., 22, 23.
Stonington, 72.
Strong, Joseph, 72.
Strong, Mistress Prudence, 10, 12.
Stryker, Gen. William S., 61.
Sullivan, 9.
Sweet, Charles, Jr., 21.
Tallmadge, Frederick S., 58.
Tarbell, Luther L., 61.
Taylor, Mrs. Charles, 22.
Taylor, Mrs. Nelson, 23.
Taylor, Mrs. William, 23.
Thomas, Hon. Mr., of Mass., 69.
Thomas, Mrs. James Y., 22, 23.
Thompson, Col., 18.
Throop, Sands, 21.
Ticonderoga, 15.
Tiernay, 71.
Trumbull, Abigail, 90.
Trumbull, David, 53, 77, 80, 88, 89.
Trumbull, Faith, Elder, 90.
Trumbull, Faith, 76.
Trumbull, Dr. Hammond, 44.
Trumbull, John (painter), 52, 76.
Trumbull, John (editor), 72.
Trumbull, Gov. Jonathan, Senr., 6, 7, 9, 12, 13, 14, 16, 25, 26, 27, 29, 32, 42, 43, 46, 47, 48, 50, 51, 52, 54, 71, 75, 79, 80, 83, 88, 89.
Trumbull, Gov. Jonathan, second, 76, 79.
Trumbull, Jonathan, 33.
Trumbull, Capt. Joseph, 75.
Trumbull, Gov. Joseph, 79.
Trumbull, Joseph (Commissary-General), 49, 76, 80.
Trumbull, Hon. Lyman, 58.
Trumbull, Mary, 76.
Trumbull Papers, 13, 14, 88.
Tucker, Edgar J., 21.

Turner, Henry E., 61.
Twichell, Joseph H., 44.
Valley Forge, 39, 78.
Van Lennep, Frederick, 61.
Virginia, 44, 87.
Wadsworth, Col., 49.
Walden, Miss, 22.
Wales, Nathaniel, Jr., 7.
Wallingford, 16.
Wanton, Governor, 47.
War Governors, 55.
War Office, 8, 9, 10, 11, 14, 18, 19, 24, 25, 26, 27, 35, 43, 48, 61, 81.
Warner, Charles Dudley, 65.
Washburn, Hon. E. B., 69.
Washington, 9, 32, 33, 42, 43, 48, 49, 50, 51, 52, 55, 56, 71, 75, 81.
Waterman, Mrs. Andrew, 22.
Watterson, Hon. Henry, 70.
Wattles, Mrs. Bethia H., 10, 11, 24, 26, 27, 33.
Webb, Gen. Alexander S., 61.
Webb, Dr. William Seward, 61.
Webb's Tavern, 81.
Wells, David A., 48.
West, Joshua, 7.
Wethersfield, 81.
Wetmore, W. A., 21.
Whitehead, Hon. John, 61.
Williams, Charles Morgan, 11, 12.
Williams, Eliphalet, 76.
Williams, Ephraim, 77.
Williams, Ezekiel, 77.
Williams, Hon. Nathaniel B., 21, 24, 26, 31.
Williams, Miss Ellen C., 22.
Williams, Solomon, 72, 76.
Williams, William, 7, 25, 72, 77, 78, 80.
Willimantic, 26.
Winchester, Mrs. Charles, 22.
Windham, 5, 8, 26.
Windham County, 71.
Winthrop, 28, 45, 54.
Woodruff, Charles H., 61.
Woodstock, 5, 72.
Yorktown, 36, 51, 81.

www.ingramcontent.com/pod-product-compliance
Lightning Source LLC
Chambersburg PA
CBHW020152170426
43199CB00010B/1009